Nick Dixon, Susan Loxley and Pau

Exam Practice
Workbook

Edexcel
GCSE Additional Science

Contents

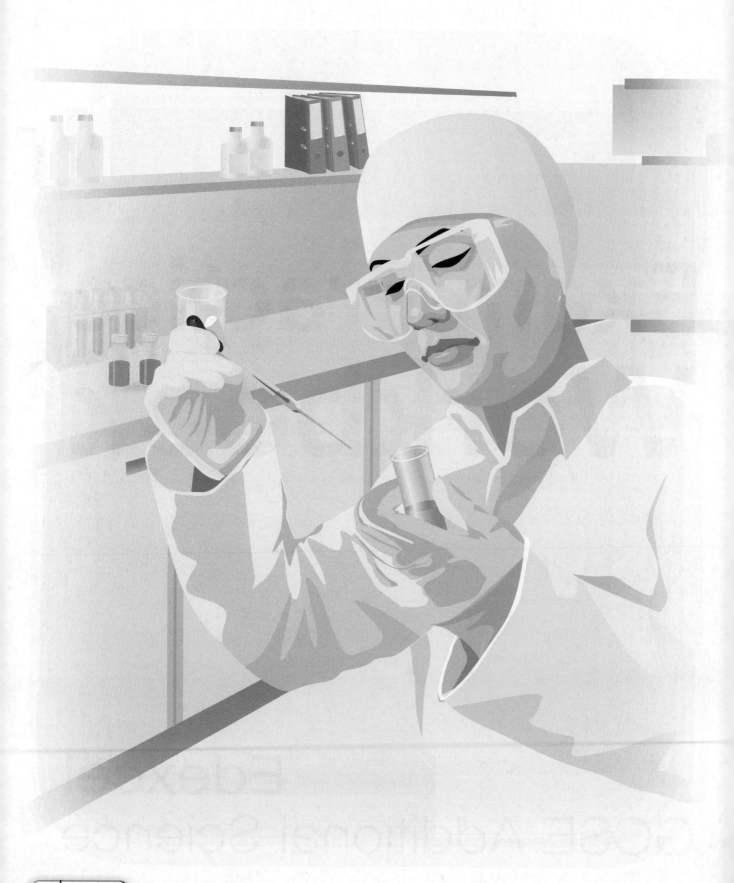

Contents

Questions labelled with an asterisk (*) are ones where the quality of your written communication will be assessed – you should take particular care with your spelling, punctuation and grammar, as well as the clarity of expression, on these questions.

1. State the difference between the way light and electron microscopes work. In your answer, identify which is more powerful. (3)

_____

_____

_____

_____

*2. Describe the similarities and differences between plant and animal cells. (6)

_____

_____

_____

_____

_____

_____

_____

_____

_____

_____

3. **(a)** State the functions of cell walls and cell membranes. (2)

_____

_____

(b) State where photosynthesis takes place in plant cells. (1)

_____

(c) Describe vacuoles in plant cells. (1)

_____

_____

4. Mitochondria are organelles found in most plant and animal cells, and are the major site of respiration.

(a) State **one** example of a type of cell likely to have many mitochondria. (1)

....

(b) Explain your choice. (1)

....

....

5. State how plasmid DNA is different from chromosomal DNA in bacteria. (1)

....

....

6. Label the parts of this bacterial cell. (4)

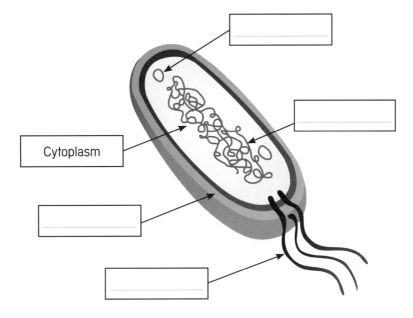

Cytoplasm

7. Chromosomes consist of long, coiled molecules of DNA.

(a) State the **two** types of human cells that do not have 23 pairs of chromosomes. (1)

....

(b) Explain why these cells only have 23 chromosomes. (1)

....

....

8. **(a)** State what genes and chromosomes are made from. (1)

(b) State the difference between genes and chromosomes. (2)

9. The structure of DNA is most accurately described as a: (1)

A ◯ double helix

B ◯ helix

C ◯ ladder

D ◯ twisted column.

10. A DNA molecule consists of two strands linked together. Describe, with the help of a diagram, the structure of DNA. (4)

11. The DNA base cytosine pairs with: (1)

A ◯ adenine

B ◯ thymine

C ◯ insulin

D ◯ guanine.

*12. Describe the process for extracting DNA from plant cells. (6)

....

....

....

....

....

....

....

....

....

....

....

....

13. **(a)** Name the **two** scientists that discovered the structure of DNA. (2)

....

(b) Name the **two** scientists that helped them in this discovery. (2)

....

(c) (i) Name the **one** scientist of the four that was not awarded the Nobel prize. (1)

....

(ii) Explain why this scientist was not awarded the Nobel prize. (1)

....

....

14. **(a)** State what genetic engineering is. (1)

....

....

(b) Describe **one** way in which bacteria have been altered in this process. (1)

....

....

15. Describe **two** applications of genetic engineering. For each example, state the organism into which the gene was inserted. Explain the benefits of this genetic engineering in your answer. (4)

....

....

....

....

....

....

16. **(a)** 'Sexual reproduction promotes variation.' Explain this sentence. (3)

....

....

....

....

(b) State how asexual reproduction is different from sexual reproduction in terms of inheriting genes. (2)

....

....

....

17. The following statements refer to mitosis. Draw a diagram to illustrate each stage. (4)

(a) Parent cell with two pairs of chromosomes → **(b)** Each chromosome replicates itself → **(c)** The copies separate and the cell divides → **(d)** Genetically identical daughter cells are formed

18. Draw straight lines to correctly match up mitosis and meiosis with **two** statements for each. (4)

| Involved in sexual reproduction |

Mitosis

Meiosis

| A diploid cell divides to produce more diploid cells |

| Produces genetically different cells |

| Needed for growth and repair |

19. Describe why meiosis must occur before fertilisation. (2)

20. How many daughter cells does meiosis produce? (1)

A ◯ One

B ◯ Two

C ◯ Four

D ◯ Eight

*21. Describe the differences between mitosis and meiosis. (6)

22. **(a)** State what a **clone** is. (1)

(b) Describe **three** of the ethical concerns about cloning. (3)

23. **(a)** State what a **stem cell** is. (1)

(b) Describe how plant and animal stems cells differ in terms of differentiation. (2)

(c) Explain why scientists think that stem cells could be very useful in the field of medicine. (1)

24. **(a)** State **three** types of specialised cells that stem cells have the potential to develop into. (3)

(b) What has to be added to stem cells to make them differentiate? (1)

25. **(a)** Explain why Parkinson's disease develops. (1)

(b) Describe how stem cell research could lead to a cure for Parkinson's disease. (2)

26. Stem cell research is controversial. Suggest **two** opposing views surrounding it. (2)

27. **(a)** What molecules are made following the instructions in DNA? (1)

(b) State **two** reasons why the body needs these molecules. (2)

28. **(a)** Describe what a DNA mutation is. Give **two** ways in which it can occur in your answer. (3)

(b) In terms of inheritance, are mutations always harmful? Explain your answer. (2)

29. **(a)** State what enzymes are also known as. (1)

(b) What do enzymes control? (1)

(c) State the general name for substances that enzymes act upon. (1)

(d) State **two** processes in the human body that involve enzymes. (2)

(e) Describe what denatured means, in terms of enzymes. (1)

30. Describe, with the help of a diagram, how the lock and key hypothesis models how enzymes work. (4)

....

....

....

....

....

....

....

....

....

31. Below is a graph that shows the effects of temperature on enzyme action.

Temperature

(a) Label the optimum temperature and maximum enzyme activity. (2)

(b) Describe what happens to the activity of the enzyme as the temperature increases up to the optimum temperature. (1)

....

(c) Describe what happens to the activity of the enzyme as the temperature increases beyond the optimum temperature. (1)

....

32. State the temperature at which enzymes in the human body work most effectively. (1)

....

33. (a) Draw a graph of how changes in pH affect enzyme action. (4)

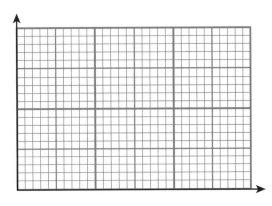

(b) Describe how changing pH affects enzyme action. (4)

....

....

....

(c) The graphs below show the action of two enzymes in the human body. Suggest which enzymes they could represent. (2)

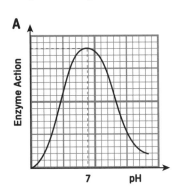

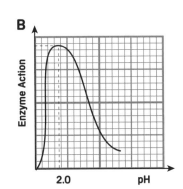

....

....

....

....

....

(Total: .... / 121)

34. (a) State what a **genome** is. (1)

....

(b) (i) Describe what the Human Genome Project achieved. (1)

....

continued...

(ii) Suggest **two** uses that might arise from the Human Genome Project. (2)

*35. Describe the stages in cloning Dolly the sheep. (6)

*36. Describe the processes of transcription and translation in protein synthesis. (6)

(Total: _____ **/ 16)**

Questions labelled with an asterisk (*) are ones where the quality of your written communication will be assessed – you should take particular care with your spelling, punctuation and grammar, as well as the clarity of expression, on these questions.

1. This is the word equation for the chemical reaction that takes place during aerobic respiration.

Glucose + Oxygen ⟶ Carbon Dioxide + Water

(a) State the balanced symbol equation for this reaction. (2)

(b) State what else is produced during aerobic respiration. (1)

(c) Describe where the glucose and oxygen come from and how they get to respiring cells. (4)

(d) State the name of the process by which reactants and products of aerobic respiration enter and leave the cells. (1)

(e) How does the body remove the **two** waste products of aerobic respiration? (2)

(f) Describe what happens to the amount of oxygen and carbon dioxide entering and leaving a muscle cell when you exercise. (2)

2. Describe respiration and ventilation. (2)

_____

_____

_____

3. Steve is running a long-distance race. A graph of his heart rate is shown below.

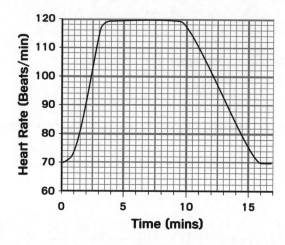

(a) Describe what happens to Steve's heart rate when he starts running the race. (1)

_____

(b) State what will happen to Steve's breathing rate. (1)

_____

(c) Explain your answers to parts **(a)** and **(b)**, using your knowledge of aerobic respiration. (4)

_____

_____

_____

_____

4. Nicole is playing football. She sprints the length of the pitch to score a goal. However, she can barely celebrate because her legs have gone weak and rubbery and she can't get her breath back. Nicole has been respiring anaerobically.

(a) State the word equation for this type of respiration. (2)

_____

(b) Explain why Nicole's legs felt rubbery. (2)

_____

_____

_____

5. State which method of respiration is the most efficient. (1)

_____

6. **(a)** When does excess post-exercise oxygen consumption occur? (1)

_____

(b) Explain why deep breathing occurs during post-exercise oxygen consumption. (2)

_____

_____

7. **(a)** State **two** ways in which leaves are adapted to make them efficient at photosynthesis. (4)

_____

_____

_____

_____

_____

(b) Label the parts of the leaf below. Describe the function of each part. (3)

(c) State the word equation for photosynthesis. (2)

_____

(d) State **three** uses of glucose made during photosynthesis. (3)

....

....

8. In a biology lesson, William was investigating how various factors affect the rate of photosynthesis. He looked at temperature first. The results he obtained are shown below.

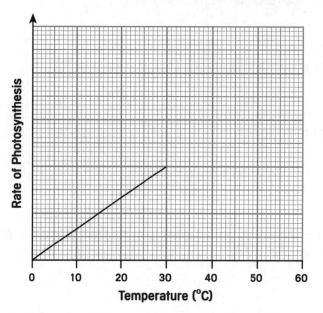

(a) He did not finish drawing the graph. Complete the graph to show the results he might have expected. (1)

(b) He then looked at how the rate of photosynthesis changed on two different days.

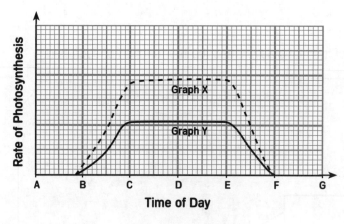

(i) State which line, X or Y, represents a warm, sunny day. (1)

....

(ii) Label the graph to show where dawn and nightfall occur. (2)

....

(iii) Describe in detail the similarities in Graph X and Graph Y in **(b)** and explain the differences between them. (4)

(c) (i) William added extra carbon dioxide to aquatic plants kept in his fish tank. He counted the bubbles of oxygen produced to determine the rate of photosynthesis.

Draw a graph to show the effects of increasing carbon dioxide on the rate of photosynthesis. Label both axes. (3)

(ii) Describe in detail what the graph in **(c) (i)** shows. (3)

9. **(a)** Explain how diffusion is different from osmosis. (2)

(b) The diagram below shows an experiment to demonstrate osmosis. Explain the results in detail. (3)

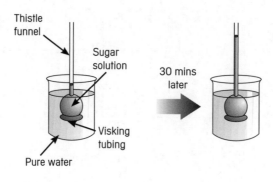

Thistle funnel

Sugar solution

30 mins later

Visking tubing

Pure water

....

....

....

....

....

(c) Which **two** of the following are examples of osmosis? (2)

A ◯ Water moving from plant cell to plant cell

B ◯ Ink spreading through water

C ◯ A potato losing water in concentrated salt solution

D ◯ Water evaporating from leaves

10. Occasionally, gardens by the sea are flooded by water. Afterwards the plants wilt and may die.
Explain why flooding with seawater causes the plants to wilt. (2)

....

....

11. **(a)** Describe the method you would use to investigate osmosis in potatoes. (4)

....

....

....

....

....

(b) Describe the results you would expect to find. (2)

_____

_____

12. **(a)** State the definition of the term **biodiversity**. (1)

_____

(b) Explain why scientists sample populations. (1)

_____

_____

(c) State the **two** groups that methods of sampling can be divided into. (2)

_____

13. Nic and Debbie's gardens back on to each other. Nic's lawn is shaded by his house, whilst Debbie's is not. They decided to investigate the differences in plant species that grew in their lawns.

(a) Describe how they would do this. Name any equipment they would use in your answer. (3)

_____

_____

_____

_____

_____

(b) State what effect using a greater number of quadrats will have on their data. (1)

_____

(c) Explain why they cannot definitely say that shade is responsible for the differences in the plants that have grown in their lawns. (3)

_____

_____

_____

_____

14. **(a)** State the major way in which plants lose water. (1)

_____

(b) Describe what a plant can do to reduce water loss. (1)

_____

(c) (i) State what process will be slowed down as a result of water loss. (1)

_____

(ii) Explain why. (1)

_____

*15. Describe water transport in plants. (6)

_____

_____

_____

_____

_____

_____

_____

_____

16. The diagram below shows an experiment investigating the water uptake by a plant. The results table is also shown below.

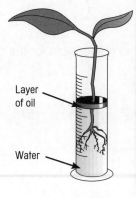

Layer of oil

Water

Time from Start (Days)	Volume of Water in Cylinder (cm³)
0	50
1	47
2	43
3	42
4	40

(a) Why is a layer of oil placed in the measuring cylinder? (1)

_____

_____

(b) Explain why the volume of water in the measuring cylinder has reduced. (1)

(c) State how you would expect the results to have changed if:

    (i) the plant had been in a colder room (1)

    (ii) the plant had been in a more humid atmosphere (1)

    (iii) air had been blown over the leaves of the plant (1)

    (iv) the plant had been placed in the sunshine. (1)

17. There are a number of other sampling methods that do not use quadrats.

    (a) Describe each of the sampling methods below.

        (i) Pitfall trap (2)

        (ii) Sweep netting (2)

        (iii) Kick sampling (2)

(b) (i) Draw and label a diagram of a pooter in the space below. (2)

(ii) Describe how it works. (1)

....

....

....

18. Describe how scientists use the mark, release, recapture method to sample mobile animals. (3)

....

....

....

....

19. Scientists closely monitor the environment.

(a) State **one** factor they might measure. (1)

....

(b) Describe why they might use electronic equipment to do this. (1)

....

(Total: .... **/ 110)**

Questions labelled with an asterisk (*) are ones where the quality of your written communication will be assessed – you should take particular care with your spelling, punctuation and grammar, as well as the clarity of expression, on these questions.

1. **(a)** State what **fossils** are. (1)

(b) State **two** reasons why the fossil record is incomplete. (2)

2. Describe the processes listed below.

(a) Cell specialisation (1)

(b) Cell elongation (1)

(c) Cell division (1)

3. **(a)** State why length and height are not accurate measurements of growth. (1)

(b) Explain why wet mass is usually used to measure growth, when dry mass is a more accurate measurement. (1)

4.   Draw graphs to show what you would expect the rate of growth for **(a)** an elephant,
     and **(b)** a redwood tree, to be over their lifetime.

(a)   **(b)**   (2)

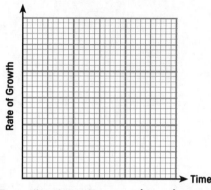

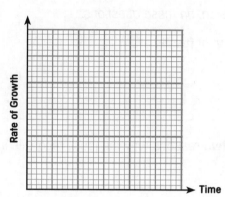

(c) Describe the difference (if any) in the shapes of your graphs.   (2)

....

....

....

5.   State **four** components of blood.

(a) ....   (1)

(b) ....   (1)

(c) ....   (1)

(d) ....   (1)

6.   Blood carries oxygen around the body.

(a) State the part of the blood that carries the oxygen.   (1)

....

(b) Describe **two** features of this part of the blood that make it well adapted to this function.   (4)

....

....

(c) Describe how blood cells carry the oxygen from the lungs to the organs in the body.   (2)

....

....

....

....

7. Describe, using diagrams to illustrate your answer, how phagocytes function. (3)

8. State the definitions of the terms **tissues**, **organs** and **systems**. (3)

9. **(a)** State the function of the circulatory system. (1)

(b) A patient has lost a lot of blood. Unless she gets more blood, her cells will die. Explain why. (1)

10. **(a)** Using the word list below label the diagram of the circulatory system. (4)

| Vena cava | Aorta | Capillaries in the lungs | Pulmonary vein |

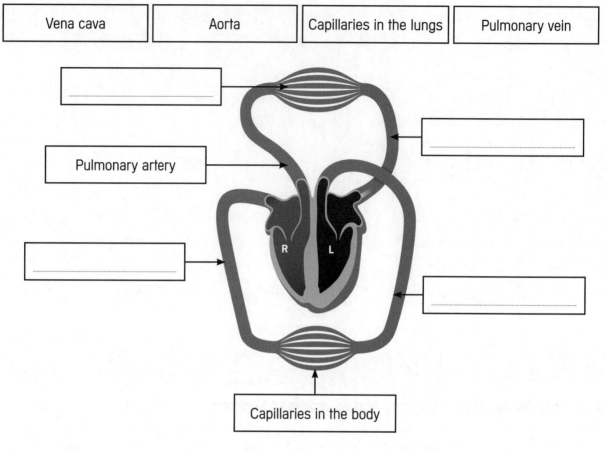

Pulmonary artery

R   L

Capillaries in the body

(b) Clearly label, with arrows, the direction of blood flow around the circulatory system on the diagram above. (4)

(c) This system is called a double circulatory system. Describe what this means. (2)

11. State the following parts of the body.

(a) The vessels that carry blood away from the heart .... (1)

(b) The place where gaseous exchange occurs .... (1)

(c) The only vein to carry oxygenated blood .... (1)

12. Label the diagram of the heart below. (4)

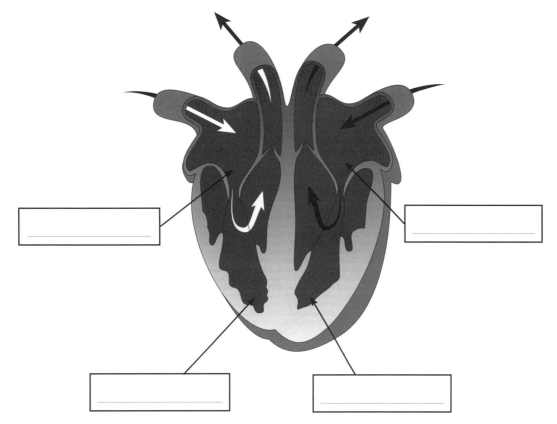

13. (a) Describe what would happen if the valve in the left side of the heart became damaged. (1)

....

(b) State what medical condition might occur if one of the blood vessels supplying the heart's muscular walls became narrowed. (1)

....

(c) State the ultimate effect that either of the above would have on a person. (1)

....

....

14. (a) Explain why the ventricles have larger and more muscular walls than the atria. (2)

....

....

(b) Explain why the left ventricle has a more muscular wall than the right ventricle. (1)

....

....

15. Rearrange the following statements into the right order so that they explain how blood is
pumped by the heart. (3)

    A The ventricles are relaxed and rapidly fill with blood.

    B The atria relax allowing blood to return to the heart from the vena cava and the pulmonary vein.

    C The ventricles contract, forcing blood out of the heart to the lungs and body.

    D The atria contract forcing blood into the ventricles through the two heart valves.

    [B] → [ ] → [ ] → [ ]

16. The diagram below shows the three types of blood vessel.

    A   **B**   **C**

    (a) State their names. (3)

        A ....   **B** ....   **C** ....

    (b) State why blood vessel **A** has a thick elastic, muscular wall. (1)

    ....

    (c) The diagram below shows a valve in a blood vessel.

        (i) State what type of blood vessel this is. .... (1)

        (ii) Draw an arrow on the diagram to show the direction of flow of the blood.
            Mark with an X the direction of the heart. (2)

        (iii) State the purpose of the valve. .... (1)

    (d) (i) State the function of blood vessel **C**. (1)

    ....

        (ii) Describe how its structure makes it well adapted for this purpose. (2)

    ....

    ....

    (e) State the name of the blood vessels that take blood away from the heart. (1)

    ....

(f) State the name of the blood vessels in which we can feel a pulse. (1)

_____

(g) State the name of the blood vessels that carry blood at high pressure. (1)

_____

17. The diagram below shows a capillary network in a muscle.

(a) Draw arrows on the diagram to show (1)
the direction of blood flow through
the muscle.

(b) Mark with an X where the blood would be (1)
rich in carbon dioxide and waste.

(c) Mark a Y where the blood would be rich in oxygen (1)
and food.

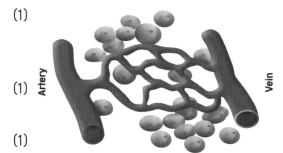

18. The diagram below shows some parts of the digestive system.

(a) Label the diagram. (4)

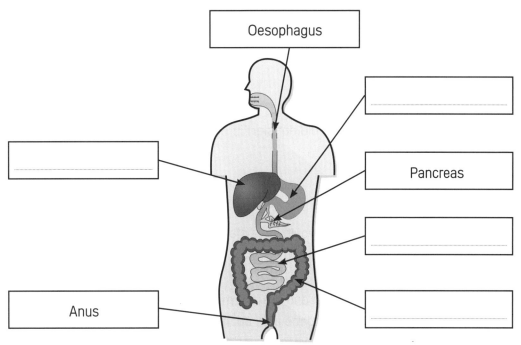

Oesophagus

Pancreas

Anus

(b) State the function of the digestive system. (1)

_____

(c) The stomach contains an acid. State **two** of the functions of acid in the stomach.

(i) _____ (1)

(ii) _____ (1)

(d) (i) George has diarrhoea. The doctor says it is due to an infection of the digestive system. State which part of George's digestive system has been affected. (1)

(ii) Explain your answer. (1)

(e) State the function of the liver in the digestive system. (1)

19. State the reactants and products that the three enzymes catalyse in the digestive system. (3)

Enzyme: ___Carbohydrase___   Reactants and products: _____

Enzyme: ___Lipase___   Reactants and products: _____

Enzyme: ___Protease___   Reactants and products: _____

20. Emily goes to a restaurant for lunch. She eats a bread roll with butter.

(a) Explain why the bread started to taste sweet after she had chewed it for a long time. (1)

(b) Explain why the digestion of butter did not start in Emily's mouth. (1)

(c) State where the digestion of butter would have started. (1)

(d) Emily also ate a hamburger in a bun and drank a milkshake. This meal is a source of protein, carbohydrate and fat. State what enzyme acts upon these substances and what they are broken down into.

(i) Protein (2)

(ii) Carbohydrate (2)

(iii) Fat (2)

21. **(a)** Explain why food molecules must be digested before they can enter the blood. (1)

*(b) Describe an experiment involving enzymes in which Visking tubing is used to model the digestive system. (6)

22. **(a)** State what **prebiotics** are. (1)

(b) What effect do they have on the digestive system? (1)

(c) Name **one** prebiotic. (1)

(Total: .... / 106)

23. Explain how the pentadactyl limb is used as evidence for evolution. (4)

24. **(a)** Some people suffer from gall stones. This condition can require the removal of the gall bladder. State the function of the gall bladder. (1)

(b) State the **two** functions of bile. (2)

*25. Villi line the small intestine. Explain how their structure aids their function. (6)

(Total: .... / 13)

Questions labelled with an asterisk (*) are ones where the quality of your written communication will be assessed – you should take particular care with your spelling, punctuation and grammar, as well as the clarity of expression, on these questions.

1. Use the information for magnesium below to answer the following questions.

mass number ➘$^{24}_{12}$Mg
atomic number ➚

    (a) What is the number of protons? _____ (1)

    (b) What is the number of electrons? _____ (1)

    (c) What is the number of neutrons? _____ (1)

    (d) Using this information, complete the electron structure for magnesium. (1)

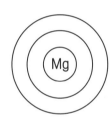

2. An element, X, has the mass number 16 and its atom contains 8 neutrons.

    (a) Calculate the number of:

        (i) protons _____ (1)

        (ii) electrons _____ (1)

    (b) Which element is X? _____ (1)

    (c) Complete the electron arrangement for this element. (1)

    (d) Which group does element X belong to? (1)

_____

    (e) Describe how your reached your answer to **(d)**. (1)

_____

3. **(a)** Complete the table below about atomic particles. (2)

Atomic Particle	Relative Mass	Relative Charge
	1	
		0
	Negligible	

(b) Describe the structure of the atom in terms of these particles. (2)

....

....

....

4. **(a)** The letters A, B, C, D, E and F represent six different elements. For each one, write: **(i)** their atomic number; **(ii)** their mass number; **(iii)** the number of protons; **(iv)** the number of electrons; **(v)** the number of neutrons in one atom. (5)

	$^{12}_{6}A$	$^{9}_{4}B$	$^{19}_{9}C$	$^{11}_{5}D$	$^{28}_{14}E$	$^{40}_{18}F$
Atomic number						
Mass number						
Number of protons						
Number of electrons						
Number of neutrons						
Name of element **(b)**						

(b) Use a periodic table to identify the elements A, B, C, D, E and F and complete the table. (3)

5. Explain what is meant by:

(a) atomic number (1)

....

(b) mass number (1)

....

*6. The diagram below shows how the element nitrogen appears on the periodic table.

mass number ➤ 14
                    N
atomic number ➤ 7

Use your knowledge of atomic structure and electron arrangement to describe how chemists are able to use this information to model atoms. (6)

....

....

....

....

....

....

....

....

....

....

....

(Total: .... / 30)

7.   **Isotope 1**   **Isotope 2**

$^{14}_{6}C$ ←— mass number —→ $^{12}_{6}C$
←— atomic number —→

(a) Describe **two** ways in which these atoms are similar.   (2)

....

....

(b) Describe **two** ways in which these atoms are different.   (2)

....

....

....

8.   **(a)** Naturally occurring chlorine contains approximately three chlorine-35 atoms to every one
        chlorine-37 atom. Use this information to calculate the relative atomic mass of chlorine.   (2)

....

....

....

(b) Naturally occurring copper contains 69% of copper-63 and 31% of copper-65. Use this
        information to calculate the relative atomic mass of copper.   (2)

....

....

....

(c) In 1000 thallium atoms, there are 705 atoms of thallium-205 and 295 atoms of
        thallium-203. Use this information to calculate the relative atomic mass of thallium.   (2)

....

....

....

(Total: .... / 10)

Questions labelled with an asterisk (*) are ones where the quality of your written communication will be assessed – you should take particular care with your spelling, punctuation and grammar, as well as the clarity of expression, on these questions.

*1. A white crystalline solid is thought to be potassium chloride.

Explain how you would identify the individual ions within the compound and confirm that the white crystalline solid is potassium chloride. (6)

....

....

....

....

....

....

....

....

....

....

2. When a solution of potassium sulfate is mixed with a solution of barium chloride, a white precipitate forms. The equation for this reaction is:

$$K_2SO_4(aq) + BaCl_2(aq) \longrightarrow BaSO_4(s) + 2KCl(aq)$$

(a) What is a precipitate? (1)

....

....

(b) Which compound is the precipitate? (1)

....

3. A precipitate will also form if magnesium sulfate is used instead of potassium sulfate. Write a word equation for this reaction. (1)

....

4. Describe a use of aqueous barium sulfate. (1)

....

....

5. **(a)** How is a precipitate separated from solution and purified? (2)

(b) When potassium sulfate is reacted with barium chloride, a precipitate is formed suspended in solution. What is left behind when the precipitate is removed? (1)

(c) How is this substance obtained as a dry solid? (1)

***6.** These labels have come off three bottles of chemicals.

Copper chloride solution $CuCl_2$(aq)	Potassium sulfate solution K_2SO_4(aq)	Copper sulfate solution $CuSO_4$(aq)

Describe and give details of the chemical tests that you would use to identify which bottle contains which substance. (6)

7. Use the information in the table to predict the formula for the following ionic compounds. Complete the table below. (6)

1+ ions	2+ ions	3+ ions	2- ions	1- ions
Lithium, Li^+	Magnesium, Mg^{2+}	Aluminium, Al^{3+}	Oxide, O^{2-}	Fluoride, F^-
Sodium, Na^+	Calcium, Ca^{2+}	Iron(III), Fe^{3+}	Sulfide, S^{2-}	Chloride, Cl^-
Potassium, K^+	Copper(II), Cu^{2+}		Sulfate, SO_4^{2-}	Bromide, Br^-
Silver, Ag^+	Iron(II), Fe^{2+}		Carbonate, CO_3^{2-}	Iodide, I^-
Ammonium, NH_4^+	Zinc, Zn^{2+}			Nitrate, NO_3^-
	Lead, Pb^{2+}			Hydroxide, OH^-

Compound	Positive Ion	Negative Ion	Formula
Zinc bromide	Zn^{2+}	Br^-	$ZnBr_2$
Silver nitrate			$AgNO_3$
Aluminium chloride			
Sodium nitrate			
Lead sulfate			
Potassium sulfate			
Copper (II) sulfate			
Calcium carbonate			
Aluminium sulfate			
Lead nitrate			
Ammonium sulfate			
Zinc nitrate			
Lead iodide			
Iron (III) oxide			

8. The statements below are simple solubility rules for chemical reactions.

All chloride salts are soluble, except for silver and lead.

All sulfate salts are soluble, except for lead, barium and calcium.

Most sodium, potassium and ammonium salts are soluble.

All carbonate salts are insoluble, except for sodium and potassium.

(a) Complete the following word equations and state which salt produced is insoluble.

    (i) Lead nitrate + Sodium sulfate ⟶ .... (1)

    (ii) Zinc sulfate + Barium chloride ⟶ .... (1)

    (iii) Copper chloride + Silver nitrate ⟶ .... (1)

(b) Using the solubility rules, decide which **two** salts you could react together to form the following.

    (i) Magnesium carbonate .... (1)

    (ii) Lead sulfate .... (1)

    (iii) Silver chloride .... (1)

(Total: .... / 32)

Higher Tier

9.   **(a)** Explain why ionic compounds have high melting points and boiling points and will conduct electricity when molten or in solution.   (3)

....

....

....

....

....

    (b) Complete the symbol equation below for the reaction between sulfate ions and barium ions to produce the white precipitate barium sulfate. (Use the periodic table to help you.)   (2)

.... (aq) + ... (aq) ⟶ .... (s)

continued...

*10. A and B are ionic substances. What does this tell you about their chemical structure and properties? (6)

_____

_____

_____

_____

_____

_____

_____

_____

_____

11. Sodium chloride is a typical ionic compound made from Na^+ ions and Cl^- ions. Use your knowledge of ionic bonding to describe the type of structure and forces you would expect this type of compound to have. (3)

_____

_____

_____

_____

(Total: _____ / 14)

Questions labelled with an asterisk (*) are ones where the quality of your written communication will be assessed – you should take particular care with your spelling, punctuation and grammar, as well as the clarity of expression, on these questions.

*1. A water molecule has the formula H_2O, which means that it contains two hydrogen atoms bonded to one oxygen atom. A hydrogen chloride molecule has the formula HCl, which means that it contains one hydrogen atom bonded to one chlorine atom. Explain, as fully as you can, why a water molecule contains two hydrogen atoms but a hydrogen chloride molecule contains one hydrogen atom. **(6)**

....

....

....

....

....

....

....

....

....

2. A student was investigating the different colours of food dye used in sweets. What technique would be the most suitable for doing this? **(1)**

....

3. What is a **molecule**? **(1)**

....

4. What is the name of the process of joining two or more non-metal atoms together? **(1)**

....

5. Why do atoms in a molecule share electrons? **(1)**

....

6. Explain how the position of an element in the periodic table can help you to determine its electron configuration. **(2)**

....

....

7.   **(a)** Referring to a periodic table, draw the structure of the atom chlorine.   (1)

   (b) How many more electrons does chlorine need in order to have a full outer shell?   (1)

   (c) How would you write the electron configuration of chlorine as numbers?   (1)

8.   Write down the electron configuration of the element in Group 5, period 2.   (1)

9.   Seven coloured substances were spotted on to a piece of filter paper, which was then stood in a covered glass tank containing a little propanone. Three of the substances were the basic colours red, blue and yellow. The others were dyes labelled A, B, C and D. The resulting chromatogram is shown below.

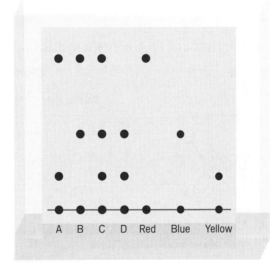

   (a) Which dye contains red, yellow and blue?   (1)

   (b) Which dye is a mixture of blue and yellow?   (1)

   (c) Why do some colours travel further than others?   (1)

10. Explain how the distance moved by the substance can be used by scientists. (2)

....

....

....

11. How are R_f values calculated? (2)

....

....

....

(Total: .... / 23)

Higher Tier

12. Give **two** properties of substances with giant covalent structures. (2)

....

....

13. The diagrams below show the structures for graphite and diamond.

Graphite

Carbon atom

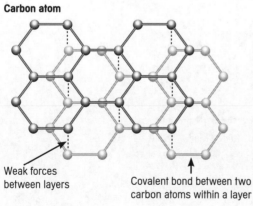

Weak forces between layers

Covalent bond between two carbon atoms within a layer

Diamond

Carbon atom

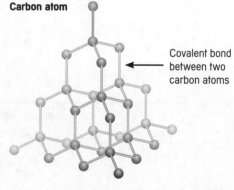

Covalent bond between two carbon atoms

(a) Name **two** differences in the structural bonding of carbon in diamond and graphite. (2)

....

....

(b) What name is used to describe the structure of the two examples above, diamond and graphite? (1)

....

continued...

14. What three properties would giant covalent structures be expected to show? (3)

A ◯ High melting point

B ◯ Low boiling point

C ◯ Giant regular structure

D ◯ Low boiling point

E ◯ High boiling point

15. Explain why the bonding within diamond allows it to be used as a cutting tool. (2)

16. Carbon dioxide is a simple molecule. Describe the bonding in this molecule and explain what is meant by the term simple molecule. You may draw a diagram to support your answer. (4)

17. Diamond and graphite have giant covalent structures. When graphite is mixed with clay, it is used as lead in pencils. Describe why pencils leave a mark on paper. (2)

(Total: _____ / 16)

Questions labelled with an asterisk (*) are ones where the quality of your written communication will be assessed – you should take particular care with your spelling, punctuation and grammar, as well as the clarity of expression, on these questions.

1. The bonding in magnesium is metallic. What does **metallic bonding** mean? Use a diagram to help with your answer. (3)

2. Use a diagram to help you explain why metals can be pulled into wires. (3)

3. Explain why a piece of iron will conduct electricity but a piece of sulfur will not. You may need to use diagrams to help you. (4)

4. Why are Group 1 metals stored under oil? (2)

5. Write a word equation for the reaction between lithium and water. (1)

6. Explain why Group 1 metals are called alkali metals. (2)

7. Reactions of potassium are more violent than reactions of lithium. Why is potassium more reactive than lithium? (2)

A ◯ Lithium is further down Group 1 than potassium

B ◯ The outer electron on potassium is further away from the nucleus than it is on lithium

C ◯ Potassium is further down Group 1 than lithium

D ◯ The outer electron on lithium is further away from the nucleus than it is on potassium

E ◯ Potassium has a higher melting point than lithium

8. Substance A has a melting point of 2300°C. When it is melted, and two electrodes connected to a bulb and battery are put into the liquid, the bulb lights up. Substance B is a liquid with a strong smell. It will not dissolve in water. (1)

(a) What type of substance is A?

(b) Which substance is made of molecules? (1)

(c) Explain why substance A conducts electricity when molten and substance B does not. (3)

9. Choose the part of the periodic table in which each element described below belongs.

Group 1	Group 2	Transition elements	Group 3	Group 4	Group 5	Group 6	Group 7	Group 8

(a) A soft metal that is shiny when cut and floats on water. _____ (1)

(b) A yellow/green gas that is used to make bleaches. _____ (1)

(c) A colourless gas used in respiration. It forms ions with 2^- charge. _____ (1)

(d) A granular metal that forms 2^+ ions. Its compounds are found in dairy products. _____ (1)

10. **(a)** Complete electron configuration diagrams for atoms of helium, neon and argon. (3)

(b) By reference to your diagrams in **(a)**, explain why the noble gases are so unreactive. (2)

....

....

11. Describe how early scientists were able to discover noble gases. (2)

....

....

12. Describe **one** use of argon and give a reason why it is used for this purpose. (2)

....

13. State **two** uses of noble gases. (2)

....

....

14. **(a)** What are **halide** ions? (1)

....

(b) Hydrogen halides will form: (1)

A ☐ alkaline gases

B ☐ insoluble gases

C ☐ colourless acidic gases

D ☐ hydrogen gas.

(c) When a hydrogen halide is dissolved in water it will form a halide ion and a .... (1)

15. Which is the more reactive of the two halogens bromine and chlorine? (1)

....

*16. Copper is a typical transition metal and is a very good conductor of electricity. The electrical connections inside a hi-fi system, for example, in a CD player or MP3 player docking station, are made from multiple strands of oxygen-free copper, which helps maintain a high signal purity. What properties of copper make it suitable for use in this situation? (6)

17. Describe what you would expect to happen:

(a) when bromine is added to a solution of sodium chloride (1)

(b) when chlorine is added to a solution of potassium iodide. (1)

18. What type of ions do metals make? Include the charge in your answer. (1)

19. What type of ions do non-metals make? Include the charge in your answer. (1)

20. Use the information about different structures, given in the table below, to identify the type of substance in the following questions.

Property	Ionic	Metallic	Simple Molecular	Giant Covalent
Melting point	High	High	Low	Very high
Boiling point	High	High	Low	Very high
Conducts electricity as a solid	Does not conduct	Conducts	Does not conduct	Does not conduct
Conducts electricity when molten	Conducts	Conducts	Does not conduct	Does not conduct
Conducts electricity in solution	Conducts	Insoluble	Usually insoluble	Insoluble
Solubility in water	Usually soluble	Insoluble	Usually insoluble	Insoluble

(a) This substance has a boiling point of 2967°C, conducts electricity as a solid and when molten, but is insoluble. _____ (1)

(b) This substance has a melting point of -7°C, does not conduct electricity as a solid or when molten, and is insoluble. _____ (1)

(c) This substance has a boiling point of 187°C, does not conduct electricity as a solid or when molten, and is insoluble. _____ (1)

(d) This substance has a boiling point of 4027°C, does not conduct electricity as a solid, and is insoluble. _____ (1)

(e) This substance has a melting point of 30°C, conducts electricity as a solid and when molten, but is insoluble. _____ (1)

(f) This substance has a boiling point of 1560°C, does not conduct electricity as a solid, but it is soluble in water. _____ (1)

21. The elements in Group 2 form ions with a double positive charge, e.g. Ca^{2+}. The elements of Group 5 form ions with a triple negative structure, e.g. N^{3-}. Explain this in terms of their electronic structure. (3)

_____

_____

_____

22. Astatine (At) is the element that is found at the bottom of Group 7.

(a) Calcium astatide is an ionic compound. Calcium ions have the formula Ca^{2+}. What is the formula of astatide ions and consequently calcium astatide? (1)

(b) Predict what would happen in the following reactions.

(i) Astatine (aq) + Potassium bromide (aq) _____ (1)

(ii) Iodine (aq) + Sodium astatide (aq) _____ (1)

(c) State the name given to the type of molecule astatine, iodine and the other Group 7 elements exist as. (1)

(Total: _____ / 64)

Higher Tier

*23. Explain, in terms of electrons, why potassium reacts so violently when compared to lithium. (6)

(Total: _____ / 6)

Questions labelled with an asterisk (*) are ones where the quality of your written communication will be assessed – you should take particular care with your spelling, punctuation and grammar, as well as the clarity of expression, on these questions.

1. Hydrogen and chlorine react together to make hydrogen chloride. This is a highly exothermic reaction. What does the term **exothermic** mean? (1)

2. The equation for the reaction between hydrogen and chlorine can be written:

    H-H + Cl-Cl $\longrightarrow$ H-Cl + H-Cl

    Which are the bonds that need to be broken? (1)

3. Is the making of bonds **exothermic** or **endothermic**? (1)

4. How do differences in bond energy between the reactants and products in a chemical reaction explain whether a reaction is exothermic? (2)

5. In catalytic converters fitted to cars, carbon monoxide and oxides of nitrogen in the exhaust are converted to other substances.

    (a) Explain why it is not desirable to leave these gases in exhaust forms. (2)

    (b) In one of the catalytic converters reactions, the nitrogen monoxide (NO) reacts with carbon monoxide to form nitrogen and carbon dioxide. Write a word equation for this reaction. (1)

6. A catalyst is used to increase the rate of chemical reaction. What is the mass of catalyst that is left at the end of the reaction if 0.5g of catalyst was added to a flask containing 100cm³ of hydrogen peroxide? (1)

Model answers have been provided for the quality of written communication questions that are marked with an asterisk (*). The model answers would score the full 6 marks available. If you have made most of the points given in the model answer and communicated your ideas clearly, in a logical sequence with few errors in spelling, punctuation and grammar, you would get 6 marks. You will lose marks if some of the points are missing, if the answer lacks clarity and if there are serious errors in spelling, punctuation and grammar.

B2 The Building Blocks of Cells (Pages 4–14)

1. Light microscopes rely on refraction of light to magnify images **(1 mark)**; Electron microscopes use beams of electrons, which have a shorter wavelength than light **(1 mark)**; Electron microscopes are therefore more powerful **(1 mark)**

*2. Plant and animal cells both possess a nucleus. Plant and animal cells both possess a cell membrane. Plant and animal cells both have a cytoplasm. Only plant cells possess a cell wall. Only plant cells possess a vacuole. Only plant cells possess chloroplasts.

3. **(a)** Cell walls provide structural support **(1 mark)**; Cell membranes control the movement of substances in and out of cells **(1 mark)**
   (b) In the chloroplasts in the green parts of plants
   (c) Large spaces in the centre of cells which are full of sap

4. **(a)** **Accept any suitable answer, e.g.** Sperm; Muscle; Liver
   (b) Because they are particularly active and need more energy generated from respiration

5. Plasmid DNA is a separate, small circular section of DNA that can replicate independently of the chromosomal DNA.

6.

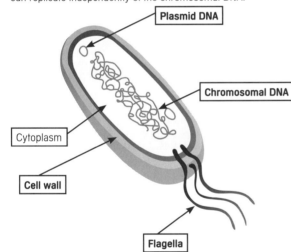

7. **(a)** Sperm and eggs
   (b) When they meet at fertilisation they join to form a cell with 23 pairs

8. **(a)** DNA
   (b) A small section of DNA that codes for a particular protein is called a gene **(1 mark)**; Many genes join together to form a chromosome **(1 mark)**

9. A **should be ticked**.

10. Two strands are held together by paired bases **(1 mark)**; The bases are adenine, thymine, cytosine and guanine **(1 mark)**; Adenine links to thymine, and cytosine links to guanine **(1 mark)**

(1 mark)

11. D **should be ticked**.

*12. Dissolve 3g of salt in 90cm³ of distilled water in a beaker and mix in 10cm³ of washing up liquid. Mash 50g of defrosted frozen peas in a second beaker with a little water and add 10cm³ of the solution to the first beaker. Place in a water bath at 60°C for 15 minutes and stir gently. Place in an ice bath for 5 minutes and stir gently. Very carefully pour chilled ethanol solution onto the top of the beaker and leave for a few minutes. The DNA will separate out into pale, bubble-covered strands at the boundary between the pea extract and the ethanol.

13. **(a)** James Watson and Francis Crick
    (b) Rosalind Franklin and Maurice Wilkins
    (c) **(i)** Rosalind Franklin
    (ii) She died before the other three scientists were awarded it (At this time the prize could only be awarded to the living)

14. **(a)** The removal of a gene from one organism and insertion into another
    (b) **Accept any suitable answer, e.g.** Bacteria have been altered to include the human gene for insulin

15. **Accept any two suitable answers, e.g.** The beta-carotene gene has been inserted into rice to reduce vitamin A deficiency in humans; The human gene for insulin has been inserted into bacteria to produce insulin for diabetics

16. **(a)** Gametes are produced when a cell divides, which 'shuffles' the genes **(1 mark)**; Gametes fuse randomly, with one of each pair of genes coming from each parent **(1 mark)**; A pair of genes may have the same alleles or different alleles, producing different characteristics **(1 mark)**
    (b) In asexual reproduction, the offspring's genes all come from the one parent, so it is genetically identical to the parent (a clone) **(1 mark)**; In sexual reproduction the offspring's genes come from both parents **(1 mark)**

17. **(a)**   **(b)**   **(c)**   **(d)**

18.

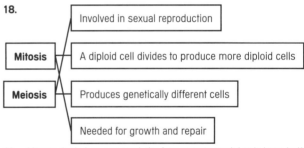

19. After meiosis has occurred, the four gamete nuclei only have half the number of chromosomes of the parental cell **(1 mark)**; During fertilisation, two gametes (one from each parent) join so the cell then contains the correct number of chromosomes **(1 mark)**

20. C **should be ticked**.

*21. Mitosis produces two daughter cells, whilst meiosis produces four. Mitosis produces genetically identical daughter cells, whilst meiosis produces different cells. Mitosis produces daughter cells with the same number of chromosomes as the parent cell. Meiosis produces daughter cells with half the number of chromosomes as the parent cell. Mitosis produces new cells for growth, to repair damaged tissues and in asexual reproduction. Meiosis produces gametes (sperm and eggs).

22. **(a)** An individual that is genetically identical to its parent
    (b) **Accept any three suitable answers, e.g.** The fear of the 'perfect race'; The possibilities of abnormalities occurring in clones; Clones will not have 'parents'; Cloning does not allow 'natural' evolution

23. **(a)** A cell which has not yet differentiated
    (b) Plant cells can differentiate at any time **(1 mark)**; Animal cells can only differentiate soon after they are made **(1 mark)**
    (c) They could replace damaged cells and tissues and help in the treatment of diseases
24. **(a) Accept any three suitable answers, e.g.** Pancreatic islet cell; Heart muscle cell; Blood cells; Neurones; Bone marrow cell
    (b) Growth factors
25. **(a)** Brain neurones are faulty (they stop producing dopamine)
    (b) Stem cells develop into neurones **(1 mark)**; If they were inserted into the brain they might produce dopamine and cure Parkinson's disease **(1 mark)**
26. **Accept any two suitable answers, e.g.** Some people think that an embryo is an individual life and so disagree with their use in stem cell research **(1 mark)**; Other people agree with the research and think it might be a cure for conditions like Parkinson's disease **(1 mark)**
27. **(a)** Proteins
    (b) Accept any two suitable answers, e.g. To make enzymes, hormones, skin, hair, etc. and for growth and repair
28. **(a)** A change to the sequence of bases that make up a gene **(1 mark)**; **Accept any two from:** UV radiation; Viruses; Some chemicals; Errors during DNA replication
    (b) Mutations are not always harmful **(1 mark)**; Some have no effect at all, whilst some are advantageous **(1 mark)**
29. **(a)** Biological catalysts
    (b) The rate of biological reactions inside living organisms
    (c) Specific substrates
    (d) Accept any two suitable answers, e.g. Digestion; Protein synthesis
    (e) It means that the enzyme is irreversibly damaged and will no longer work
30. The enzyme is the lock and the substrate is the key **(1 mark)**; The substrate enters the enzyme (like a key in a lock) **(1 mark)**; It is then broken down **(1 mark)**; The enzyme is specific for the substrate, like a lock and key **(1 mark)**

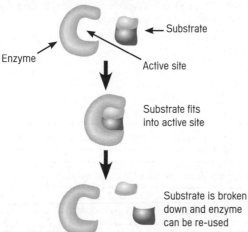

Substrate
Enzyme
Active site

Substrate fits into active site

Substrate is broken down and enzyme can be re-used

31. **(a) (1 mark for each label)**

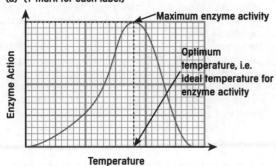

Maximum enzyme activity
Optimum temperature, i.e. ideal temperature for enzyme activity
Enzyme Action
Temperature

    (b) It increases
    (c) It decreases
32. 37°C

33.

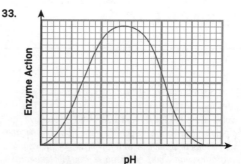

Enzyme Action
pH

    (a) 1 mark each for: correct axes; appropriate labelling of axes; appropriately shaped graph; smooth curve
    (b) When the pH is low the enzyme action is low **(1 mark)**; As the pH increases so does the enzyme action, until the optimum is reached **(1 mark)**; Further increases in pH result in a decrease in enzyme action **(1 mark)**; There is no enzyme action at extreme high or low pH **(1 mark)**
    (c) A: Amylase; B: Protease
34. **(a)** All the genetic material in an organism
    (b) (i) It identified the sequence of all bases in every gene of the human genome
        (ii) Accept any two suitable answers, e.g. To identify and replace 'faulty' genes; To compare DNA samples from potential suspects at crime scenes
*35. The diploid nucleus is taken from a mature cell (ordinary body cell) of the donor organism. The diploid nucleus, containing all of the donor's genetic information, is inserted into an empty egg cell (i.e. an egg cell with the nucleus removed or enucleated). This is nuclear transfer. The egg cell, containing the diploid nucleus, is stimulated so that it begins to divide by mitosis. The resulting embryo is implanted in the uterus of a 'surrogate mother'. The embryo develops into a foetus and is born as normal.
*36. Transcription begins when the DNA of the gene that codes for the protein to be copied unzips. mRNA copies the base pair sequence of this gene. mRNA exits the nuclear membrane into the cytoplasm.
    Translation then begins when the mRNA attaches to a ribosome. tRNA molecules align opposite the mRNA, each bringing with them an amino acid. The amino acids form to make a polypeptide, and then a protein.

B2 Organisms and Energy (Pages 15–24)

1. **(a) (1 mark for reactants, 1 mark for products)**
        $C_6H_{12}O_6 + 6O_2 \longrightarrow 6CO_2 + 6H_2O$
    (b) Energy
    (c) Glucose is obtained from food **(1 mark)**; Oxygen is taken in from the air **(1 mark)**; They are transported in the blood **(1 mark)**; Glucose and oxygen move from the capillaries into the respiring cells by diffusion **(1 mark)**
    (d) Diffusion
    (e) Carbon dioxide is breathed out **(1 mark)**; Water is lost as sweat, moist breath or excreted as urine **(1 mark)**
    (f) More oxygen is absorbed into the muscle cell by diffusion from the capillaries **(1 mark)**; More carbon dioxide is removed by diffusion from the muscle cell into the capillaries **(1 mark)**
2. Respiration is the breakdown of glucose to create energy **(1 mark)**; Ventilation is breathing (This is the process of getting oxygen into and carbon dioxide out of the lungs) **(1 mark)**
3. **(a)** It increases
    (b) It will increase
    (c) The breathing rate increases so that more oxygen can be taken in **(1 mark)**; The cells need more oxygen because they are respiring faster **(1 mark)**; This means more carbon dioxide needs to be removed **(1 mark)**; As both these gases are transported in the blood, the heart rate also increases **(1 mark)**
4. **(a) (1 mark for reactant, 1 mark for product)**
        Glucose $\longrightarrow$ Lactic acid
    (b) Not enough oxygen can reach her muscle cells, which means she respires anaerobically **(1 mark)**; Glucose is broken down into lactic acid, a waste product which builds up in her muscles and causes them to feel rubbery **(1 mark)**

5. Aerobic respiration
6. **(a)** When muscle cells have been respiring anaerobically (usually after strenuous exercise)
   (b) Lactic acid needs to be broken down into carbon dioxide and water **(1 mark)**; Deep breathing continues after exercise to provide the oxygen to do this **(1 mark)**
7. **(a)** **Accept any two suitable answers, e.g.** Leaves have lots of internal air spaces to create a large surface area for gas exchange; Leaves are full of chloroplasts containing chlorophyll for photosynthesis; Leaves are flat to absorb as much sunlight as possible.
   (b)

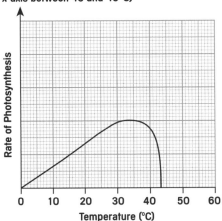

A waxy layer on the top of the leaf stops transpiration

Palisade cells contain lots of chloroplasts for photosynthesis

Stomata are small pores found mainly on the underside of plant leaves

   (c) **(1 mark for reactants, 1 mark for products)**
   $$\text{Carbon dioxide + Water} \xrightarrow[\text{chlorophyll}]{\text{light}} \text{Glucose + Oxygen}$$
   (d) **Accept any three from:** Used in respiration; Stored as starch; Made into cellulose cell walls; Made into proteins
8. **(a)** **(Award 1 mark for any line that falls steeply and meets the x-axis between 40 and 45°C)**

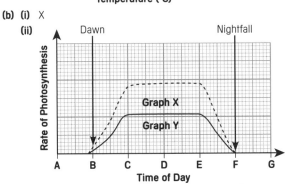

   (b) (i) X
   (ii)

Dawn   Nightfall

Graph X

Graph Y

A   B   C   D   E   F   G
Time of Day

   (iii) As the levels of light increased in the morning (between points B and C) so did the rate of photosynthesis **(1 mark)**; At approximately point C the rate reached a maximum and continued until the sun began to set **(1 mark)**; At this point the rate of photosynthesis decreased (between E and F) to zero **(1 mark)**; On a warm, sunny day a higher maximum of photosynthesis rate was observed **(1 mark)**

(c) (i) **(1 mark each for: correct axes; appropriately shaped graph; smooth curve)**

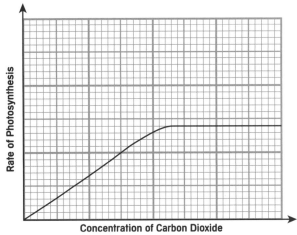

Concentration of Carbon Dioxide

   (ii) When the concentration of carbon dioxide was low, so was the rate of photosynthesis **(1 mark)**; As the concentration increased, so did the rate of photosynthesis until a maximum was reached **(1 mark)**; After this, further increases in carbon dioxide had no effect on the rate of photosynthesis **(1 mark)**
9. **(a)** Diffusion is the movement of any substance; Osmosis is the movement of water **(1 mark)**; Osmosis occurs across a partially permeable membrane; diffusion doesn't **(1 mark)**
   (b) The sugar solution in the thistle funnel has a lower concentration of water than the beaker **(1 mark)**; As a consequence, water moves from the beaker into the thistle funnel across the Visking tubing **(1 mark)**; This forces the water higher up the tube **(1 mark)**
   (c) A and C should be ticked.
10. When the plants are surrounded by salt water there is a higher concentration of water in their cells than the salt water **(1 mark)**; Therefore, water diffuses from their cells causing them to wilt and perhaps die **(1 mark)**
11. **(a)** **Accept any suitable answer, e.g.** Cut out, dry off and measure accurately the mass of some small pieces of potato **(1 mark)**; Place one in a beaker of distilled water for 15 minutes **(1 mark)**; Remove, dry off the potato and measure its mass again **(1 mark)**; Repeat the process using various concentrations of sugar solution **(1 mark)**
   (b) The potato in the beaker of distilled water should have gained mass as water entered it by osmosis **(1 mark)**; The potato in the sugar solutions should have lost mass as water left it by osmosis. (Unless one solution is the same concentration as the potato in which case no mass would be lost) **(1 mark)**
12. **(a)** A measure of the variety of different organisms in a habitat
   (b) Because sampling entire populations is inefficient or sometimes impossible
   (c) Systematic **(1 mark)**; random **(1 mark)**
13. **(a)** **Accept any suitable answer, e.g.** They would use quadrats to sample their lawns **(1 mark)**; They could place their quadrat randomly on their lawns and count the numbers of different species of plant that grew in them **(1 mark)**; This would determine the species richness or frequency **(1 mark)**
   (b) Make it more reliable
   (c) There are many variables that affect how lawns grow besides shade **(1 mark)**; **Accept any two suitable answers, e.g.** The amount of water they receive; The quality of the soil
14. **(a)** Evaporation through pores in their leaves called stomata
   (b) Make their stomata smaller
   (c) (i) Photosynthesis will be slowed down
       (ii) Water is a reactant so less of it means less reaction occurs
*15. Water evaporates from the internal leaf cells through the stomata. Water passes from the xylem vessels to leaf cells due to osmosis. This 'pulls' the entire 'thread' of water in that vessel upwards by a very small amount. Water enters the xylem from the root tissue to replace water which has moved upwards. Water enters root hair cells by osmosis to replace water which has entered the xylem.

16. **(a)** To stop water evaporating from it
    (b) It has evaporated from the plant's leaves
    (c) (i) There would be less transpiration so less water lost
        (ii) There would be less transpiration so less water lost
        (iii) There would be more transpiration so more water lost
        (iv) There would be more transpiration so more water lost
17. **(a) (i)** Pitfall traps are small containers buried in the ground to catch small animals **(1 mark)**; They sometimes contain food to attract the small animals that fall in and are caught **(1 mark)**
        (ii) Sweep netting uses a large net **(1 mark)**; which is swept through undergrowth to catch insects **(1 mark)**
        (iii) Kick sampling involves placing a net downstream of an area of stream bed that is gently disturbed **(1 mark)**; to catch animals swept downstream **(1 mark)**
    (b) (i) **(1 mark for diagram, 1 mark for labels)**

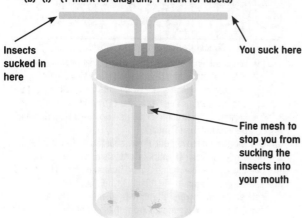

Insects sucked in here

You suck here

Fine mesh to stop you from sucking the insects into your mouth

        (ii) When one tube is sucked insects are pulled through the other tube into the jar (not the person's mouth)
18. Organisms are caught and marked in a way that will not harm them **(1 mark)**; They are then freed to be caught again during random sampling **(1 mark)**; The number caught that are marked, compared with the number unmarked, can be used to estimate the total population **(1 mark)**
19. **(a) Accept any suitable answer, e.g.** Temperature, pH, light intensity
    (b) Accept any suitable answers, e.g. It can take measurements more frequently or accurately

B2 Common Systems (Pages 25–34)

1. **(a)** The imprints or remains of plants and animals from millions of years ago, preserved in sedimentary rocks
   (b) Accept any two from: Not all fossils have been discovered yet; Some body parts are not fossilised; Fossilisation does not always occur
2. **(a) Specialisation:** the process through which an unspecialised cell becomes a specific type of cell
   (b) Elongation: the process by which cells elongate (stretch out)
   (c) Division: the process by which two cells are formed from one cell (mitosis)
3. **(a)** They do not take into account growth in other directions
   (b) Because dry mass can only be measured when the organism is dead
4. **(a)**

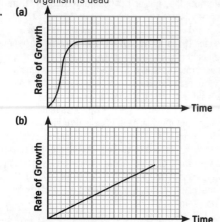

   (b)

(c) In the first graph, the growth rate is fast to begin with, then it slows down and stops **(1 mark)**; In the second graph, the growth rate is constant **(1 mark)**
5. **In any order:**
   (a) Red blood cells **(b)** White blood cells **(c)** Plasma
   (d) Platelets
6. **(a)** Red blood cells
   (b) (1 mark for each feature, 1 mark for each adaptation)
       Biconcave shape provides a large surface area through which to absorb oxygen; No nucleus so cells can (hold more haemoglobin and) carry more oxygen
   (c) Accept any suitable answer, e.g. In the lungs haemoglobin in the red blood cells combines with oxygen to form oxyhaemoglobin **(1 mark)**; The blood travels round the body through the arteries, delivering the oxygen to tissues/organs **(1 mark)**
7. **(1 mark for diagram, 2 marks for suitable description)**

White blood cell (phagocyte)

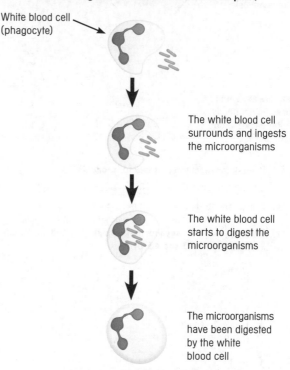

The white blood cell surrounds and ingests the microorganisms

The white blood cell starts to digest the microorganisms

The microorganisms have been digested by the white blood cell

8. Tissues are groups of the same specialised cells that complete the same function **(1 mark)**; Organs are groups of tissues that are joined together to complete a specific function **(1 mark)**; Systems are groups of organs that work together to complete a specific function **(1 mark)**
9. **(a)** It is responsible for transporting carbon dioxide, oxygen, nutrients, waste products and hormones around the body
   (b) Without oxygen cells cannot respire and produce energy
10. **(a–b)**

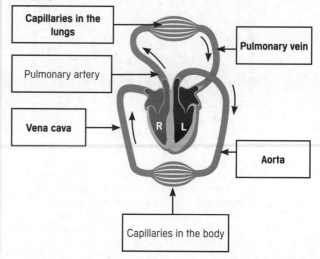

Capillaries in the lungs

Pulmonary vein

Pulmonary artery

Vena cava

R L

Aorta

Capillaries in the body

(c) The blood passes through the heart twice on a journey around the body **(1 mark)**; It goes from the heart to the lungs, to the heart and to the rest of the body before returning to the heart **(1 mark)**

11. **(a)** Arteries
    (b) Lungs
    (c) Pulmonary vein

12.

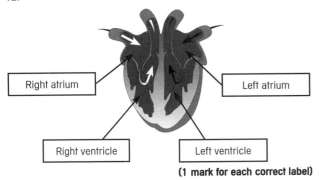

Right atrium

Left atrium

Right ventricle

Left ventricle

(1 mark for each correct label)

13. **(a)** Blood would not be pumped as effectively to the body
    (b) Coronary heart disease (or a heart attack)
    (c) Death

14. **(a)** Because ventricles need to pump the blood to the lungs and rest of body **(1 mark)**; Atria just need to pump blood to the ventricles **(1 mark)**
    (b) Because the left ventricle needs to pump blood further (to the body) than the right ventricle (to the lungs)

15. **In this order:** D, A, C

16. **(a)** A is an artery; B is a vein; C is a capillary
    (b) To cope with blood under high pressure as it has just been pumped from the heart
    (c) (i) A vein
        (ii) Arrow pointing upwards **(1 mark)**; Cross above diagram **(1 mark)**
        (iii) To stop blood flowing backwards
    (d) (i) To take blood into tissues for exchange of substances
        (ii) **(1 mark for structure, 1 mark for function)** Their narrow, thin walls allow substances to diffuse easily
    (e) Arteries
    (f) Arteries
    (g) Arteries

17. **(a)-(c)**

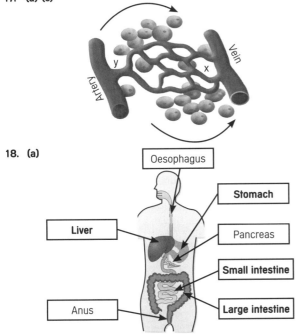

Artery

Vein

y

x

18. **(a)**

Oesophagus

Stomach

Liver

Pancreas

Small intestine

Anus

Large intestine

(1 mark for each correct label)
    (b) To break down large insoluble molecules (food) into smaller ones which can be absorbed into the blood
    (c) (i)–(ii) In either order: Provides the correct pH for protease enzymes to work; Kills bacteria

(d) (i) Large intestine
    (ii) Because the large intestine absorbs water, so diarrhoea results from a problem with this organ
(e) To produce bile which helps break down fats

19. Enzyme: Carbohydrase   Reactants and products: Breaks down carbohydrates into sugars **(1 mark)**
    Enzyme: Lipase   Reactants and products: Breaks down fats into fatty acids and glycerol **(1 mark)**
    Enzyme: Protease   Reactants and products: Breaks down proteins into amino acids **(1 mark)**

20. **(a)** The carbohydrase enzyme (amylase) in her saliva broke the carbohydrate in the bread down into sugars
    (b) Saliva in the mouth only contains carbohydrase and not lipase to break down fats (butter)
    (c) In the small intestine
    (d) (i) Protein is broken down into amino acids **(1 mark)** by proteases **(1 mark)**
        (ii) Carbohydrates are broken down into sugars **(1 mark)** by carbohydrases **(1 mark)**
        (iii) Fats are broken down into fatty acids and glycerol **(1 mark)** by lipases **(1 mark)**

21. **(a)** Because food is made of large, insoluble molecules which need to be broken down into smaller, soluble ones before they can be absorbed
    *(b) Fill a short length of Visking tubing with starch and place in a beaker of water. Test the surrounding water solution with iodine to prove that starch cannot pass through. Fill a second short length of Visking tubing with starch and add some amylase enzyme before placing in a beaker of water. (The amylase should break down the starch into glucose.) Test the surrounding water solution again with iodine to prove that starch cannot pass through. Test the water for glucose using Benedict's solution to prove that glucose can pass through.

22. **(a)** Non-digestible, functional foods
    (b) They stimulate the growth of useful bacteria in the intestines
    (c) Accept any suitable answer, e.g. Oligosaccharides

23. The pentadactyl limb is a pattern of limb bones found in all classes of vertebrates with four legs (tetrapods) **(1 mark)**; It includes one proximal bone, two distal bones, several carpals, five metacarpals, and many phalanges **(1 mark)**; Animals have evolved different arrangements of these bones **(1 mark)**; The similarity of this arrangement in all tetrapods indicates that they have evolved from a single ancestor **(1 mark)**

24. **(a)** It stores the bile made by the liver
    (b) Bile neutralises stomach acid **(1 mark)**; Bile emulsifies fat **(1 mark)**

*25. Villi are small finger-like projections that cover the walls of the small intestine. They massively increase the surface area of the intestine. They have a huge blood supply. They are only one cell thick. This allows efficient absorption of small, soluble molecules into the blood.

C2 Atomic Structure and the Periodic Table (Pages 35–38)

1. **(a)** 12 *the same as the atomic number*
   (b) 12 *the same as the number of protons*
   (c) 12 *mass number – atomic number*
   (d)

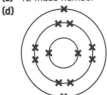

2. **(a) (i)** 8
       (ii) 8
   (b) Oxygen
   (c)

(d) Group 6

(e) Six electrons on the outer shell

3. (a)

Atomic Particle	Relative Mass	Relative Charge
Proton	1	+1
Neutron	1	0
Electron	Negligible	−1

(1 mark for atomic particles; 1 mark for relative mass and relative charge)

(b) Nucleus in centre of atom containing neutral neutrons and positively charged protons **(1 mark)** surrounded by negatively charged electrons arranged in different shells/orbit energy levels **(1 mark)**

4. (a) **(1 mark for each complete row)**

(b) **(6 correct names = 3 marks; 4–5 correct = 2 marks; 2–3 correct = 1 mark)**

	$^{12}_{6}A$	$^{9}_{4}B$	$^{19}_{9}C$	$^{11}_{5}D$	$^{28}_{14}E$	$^{40}_{18}F$
Atomic number	6	4	9	5	14	18
Mass number	12	9	19	11	28	40
Number of protons	6	4	9	5	14	18
Number of electrons	6	4	9	5	14	18
Number of neutrons	6	5	10	6	14	22
Name of element **(b)**	Carbon	Beryllium	Fluorine	Boron	Silicon	Argon

5. (a) Number of protons in an atom (or electrons)

(b) Total number of protons and neutrons in the nucleus

*6. The atoms of the elements on the periodic table have two numbers, an atomic number and a mass number. The mass number is the number of protons and neutrons in the nucleus of the atom and will also show if there are isotopes of the element. The atomic number is the number of protons or electrons and is often referred to as the proton number. It is also the number that is used to order the elements in the periodic table. The number of protons within an atom is the same as the number of electrons because the protons are positively charged and the electrons are negatively charged. Atoms have an overall neutral charge, neither negative nor positive. The proton number or atomic number help you to work out the electronic arrangement in an atom. This is because there is exactly the same the number of electrons to protons in any given neutral atom. The electronic arrangement can be used to describe how an element reacts and to show different types of chemical bonding, e.g. covalent bonding, ionic bonding and metallic bonding.

7. (a) **Accept any two from:** They have the same chemical properties; Same number of protons; Same number of electrons

(b) They have different number of neutrons in their nuclei **(1 mark)**; They have different masses **(1 mark)**

8. (a) For every 100 atoms Cl-35 = 75 atoms and Cl-37 = 25 atoms
Total mass for 100 atoms = (75 × 35) + (25 × 37) = 2625 + 925 = 3550 **(1 mark)**

Average mass for chlorine = $\frac{3550}{100}$ = 35.5 **(1 mark)**

(b) For every 100 atoms Cu-63 = 69 atoms and Cu-65 = 31 atoms
Total mass for 100 atoms = (69 × 63) + (31 × 65) = 4347 + 2015 = 6362 **(1 mark)**

Average mass for copper = $\frac{6362}{100}$ = 63.62 **(1 mark)**

(c) Total mass for 1000 atoms = (705 × 205) + (295 × 203) = 144 525 + 59 885 = 204 410 **(1 mark)**

Average mass for thallium = $\frac{204\ 410}{1000}$ = 204.41 **(1 mark)**

C2 Ionic Compounds and Analysis (Pages 39–43)

*1. The initial test would be a flame test to identify the metal ion present within the compound. Use a nichrome wire dipped in hydrochloric acid and then into the solid compound. If when placed into a blue flame, a lilac flame shows, then this lilac flame indicates the presence of a potassium ion. The next step is to test for the non-metal ion. The compound is dissolved in distilled water to form a solution. A small amount of the solution is then acidified with nitric acid. Into this acidified solution, a small amount of silver nitrate solution is added. If a white precipitate forms, then the chloride ion is present. These two tests would confirm that the white crystalline solid is potassium chloride.

2. (a) A solid which forms when two aqueous solutions react to make an insoluble product.

(b) Barium sulfate

3. Magnesium sulfate + Barium chloride ⟶ Barium sulfate + Magnesium chloride

4. For X-rays of digestive system – as barium meals

5. (a) Filtered **(1 mark)** then washed with distilled water **(1 mark)**

(b) A salt solution such as potassium chloride

(c) Water is evaporated off

*6. A flame test will identify the metal – a green-blue flame is copper and a lilac flame is potassium. Take a small amount of each solution, add nitric acid, then silver nitrate. If a white precipitate is formed, then chloride ions are present and the solution is copper(II) chloride. Take a small amount of the remaining solutions, add hydrochloric acid, then barium chloride. If a white precipitate forms then barium sulfate has formed and the solution contains sulfate ions. So if the solution produces a white precipitate and a green-blue flame it is copper sulfate. If the solution produces a white precipitate and a lilac flame it is potassium sulfate.

7.

Zinc bromide	Zn^{2+}	Br^-	$ZnBr_2$
Silver nitrate	Ag^+	NO_3^-	$AgNO_3$
Aluminium chloride	Al^{3+}	Cl^-	$AlCl_3$
Sodium nitrate	Na^+	NO_3^-	$NaNO_3$
Lead sulfate	Pb^{2+}	SO_4^{2-}	$PbSO_4$
Potassium sulfate	K^+	SO_4^{2-}	K_2SO_4
Copper(II) sulfate	Cu^{2+}	SO_4^{2-}	$CuSO_4$
Calcium carbonate	Ca^{2+}	CO_3^{2-}	$CaCO_3$
Aluminium sulfate	Al^{3+}	SO_4^{2-}	$Al_2(SO_4)_3$
Lead nitrate	Pb^{2+}	NO_3^-	$Pb(NO_3)_2$
Ammonium sulfate	NH_4^+	SO_4^{2-}	$(NH_4)_2SO_4$
Zinc nitrate	Zn^{2+}	NO_3^-	$Zn(NO_3)_2$
Lead iodide	Pb^{2+}	I^-	PbI_2
Iron(III) oxide	Fe^{3+}	O^{2-}	Fe_2O_3

(12 correct = 6 marks; 10–11 correct = 5 marks; 8–9 correct = 4 marks; 6–7 correct = 3 marks; 4–5 correct = 2 marks; 2–3 correct = 1 mark)

8. (a) (i) Lead sulfate (insoluble) + Sodium nitrate
(ii) Zinc chloride + Barium sulfate (insoluble)
(iii) Copper nitrate + Silver chloride (insoluble)

(b) (i) Magnesium nitrate/sulfate/chloride + potassium/sodium carbonate
(ii) Lead nitrate + sodium/potassium sulfate
(iii) Silver nitrate + any metal chloride (except lead)

9. (a) Structure is a giant lattice arrangement of positive ions and negative ions **(1 mark)**; Strong electrostatic forces of attraction hold the anions and cations together and lots of energy is needed to break the forces **(1 mark)**; When molten or in solution, the ions are free to move and therefore they can conduct electricity **(1 mark)**

(b) **(1 mark for correct ions; 1 mark for formula):**
$SO_4^{2-}(aq) + Ba^{2+}(aq) \longrightarrow BaSO_4(s)$

*10. The ionic substances A and B contain a positive metal ion and a negative non-metal ion. Metals form positive ions because they donate their outer electrons to non-metals in order to achieve a complete outer shell. The non-metals become negative ions because they accept these donated electrons to complete their outer shell. These oppositely charged ions are attracted to each other and will arrange themselves in a regular crystalline structure. The ions are held together in their arrangement by strong electrostatic forces of attraction between positive ions/cations and negative ions/anions. By being attracted to each other, the positive ions/cations and negative ions/anions now form a neutral charged compound. They will have high melting points and boiling points and conduct electricity when molten or in solution.

11. Sodium ions and chlorine ions are in a regular arrangement **(1 mark)**; They are held together by strong electrostatic forces **(1 mark)**; These forces are between the oppositely charged ions and form the ionic bond **(1 mark)**

C2 Covalent Compounds and Separation Techniques (Pages 44–47)

*1. Both hydrogen chloride and water contain hydrogen atoms. Hydrogen needs 1 electron to achieve a full outermost shell. In hydrogen chloride there is only 1 hydrogen atom because chlorine also needs 1 electron to achieve a full outermost shell so both the hydrogen and chlorine can achieve their full outermost shells by sharing 1 electron each. In water there are 2 hydrogen atoms because oxygen needs 2 electrons to achieve a full outermost shell so oxygen shares 1 electron each with two hydrogen atoms. By sharing 1 electron each with two hydrogen atoms both the oxygen and the hydrogen atoms achieve full outermost shells.

2. Chromatography

3. Two or more atoms joined together chemically

4. Covalent bonding

5. To gain full outer shells

6. Period = number of energy levels/shells **(1 mark)**; Group = number of electrons in outer energy level/shells **(1 mark)**

7. **(a)**

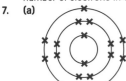

   (b) 1   **(c)** 2. 8. 7

8. 2.5

9. **(a)** C   **(b)** D

   (c) The distance travelled by a dye is determined by the solvent and the characteristics of the support

10. To calculate the R_f value of a substance **(1 mark)** and identify it by comparing the answer to known results **(1 mark)**

11. Distance moved by substance **(1 mark)** divided by distance moved by solvent **(1 mark)**

12. **Accept any two from:** High boiling point; High melting point; Do not conduct electricity; Insoluble

13. **(a)** **Accept any two from:** Carbon atoms in diamond are covalently bonded to four other carbon atoms; carbon atoms in graphite are bonded to three other carbon atoms with a free electron; Diamond has strong intramolecular forces, graphite has weak intermolecular forces; Graphite conducts electricity.

   (b) Giant covalent molecule

14. A, C **and** E **should be ticked.**

15. Rigid covalent bonds between atoms keep the diamond in a regular crystalline structure **(1 mark)**; Bonding makes diamond an extremely hard substance so the cutting edge will not wear away **(1 mark)**

16. Carbon dioxide CO_2 C=O=C **(1 mark)**

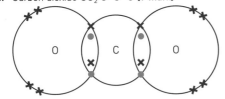

Carbon has four electrons in the outer shell, accepts two from each oxygen to make a total of eight electrons **(1 mark)**; Oxygen has six electrons in the outer shell and accepts two from the Carbon to make a total of eight electrons **(1 mark)**; This creates two carbon-oxygen double bonds and the three atoms form a small molecule **(1 mark)**

17. Carbon atoms in graphite form layers **(1 mark)**; Layers will rub off onto the paper **(1 mark)**

C2 Groups in the Periodic Table (Pages 48–53)

1.

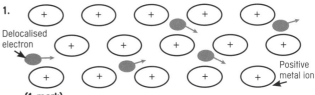

(1 mark)

Outermost electrons on each atom becomes delocalised **(1 mark)**; Positive metal atoms are held in their regular structure by a sea of these delocalised electrons **(1 mark)**

2. Atoms in a metal form regular layers **(1 mark)**; As the metal is drawn the layers slide over each other and line up **(1 mark)** **(1 mark for similar diagram to question 1)**

3. Iron contains delocalised electrons that are free to move and carry electricity **(1 mark)**; Sulfur is a non-metal. Non-metals are unable to conduct electricity because they have no delocalised / free electrons moving about their structure **(1 mark)**. Free-moving electrons are needed for electricity to flow **(1 mark)**. (However the non-metal carbon in the form of graphite is the only non-metal able to conduct electricity because it has free moving electrons.) **(1 mark for similar diagram to question 1)**

4. To prevent water getting to the metal **(1 mark)**; To prevent oxygen from air reacting with the metal **(1 mark)**

5. Lithium + Water ⟶ Lithium hydroxide + Hydrogen

6. They react to form oxides and hydroxides **(1 mark)**, which are soluble in water to form alkaline solutions **(1 mark)**

7. B **and** C **should be ticked.**

8. **(a)** Ionic **(b)** Substance B

   (c) Ionic made of positive and negative ions **(1 mark)**; Covalent molecules do not form ions so are unable to conduct electricity **(1 mark)**; Break down when molten and become free to move between electrodes **(1 mark)**

9. **(a)** Group 1 **(b)** Group 7 **(c)** Group 6 **(d)** Group 2

10. **(a)**   (3)

   (3 marks – 1 for each diagram)

   (b) Full **(1 mark)**; Complete outer shells/Energy levels **(1 mark)**

11. Visible spectrum **(1 mark)** and measuring density of air **(1 mark)**

12. **(1 mark for use, 1 mark for reason)** Light bulb; It is unreactive and provides an inert atmosphere; Welding; It acts like a shield around the weld until metal cools preventing any reaction with oxygen.

13. **Accept any two from:** Balloons; Airships; Light bulbs; Electric discharge tubes

14. **(a)** Ions of Group 7 atoms

   (b) C **should be ticked.**

   (c) Hydrogen ions

15. Chlorine

*16. Copper is suitable for electrical wiring through a combination of both physical and chemical properties. The physical properties are its metallic structure where the metal atoms are arranged into layers and grains. These layers make the copper ductile meaning that it can be drawn into wires. It is also malleable, meaning it can be bent easily to form connectors between wires. The grains in the crystalline structure make it strong and durable so that the wires will not wear out. The metallic bonding provides the delocalised electrons that are free to move around the structure of the metal, and so allow copper to conduct electricity well. It is therefore important that the copper remains oxygen-free, as any oxygen present within the structure will disrupt the movement of electrons and interfere with the metal's ability to conduct electricity.

17. (a) Nothing
    (b) Chlorine will displace iodide ions from solution and form potassium chloride; iodine solid will be precipitated
18. Positively charged (Cation)
19. Negatively charged (Anion)
20. (a) Metallic
    (b) Simple molecular
    (c) Simple molecular
    (d) Giant covalent
    (e) Metallic
    (f) Ionic
21. Elements will either gain electrons or lose electrons to achieve a stable full outer shell (1 mark); Group 2 elements have two electrons in their outer shell which they lose to become 2+ ions (1 mark); Group 5 elements have five electrons in their outer shell and need to gain three more so become 3- ions (1 mark)
22. (a) At⁻; CaAt₂
    (b) (i) Nothing
        (ii) Sodium iodide + astatine (displacement reaction)
    (c) Diatomic
23. When an alkali metal reacts it loses the only outer electron to form a single positive charged ion and as you go down Group 1 the atomic radius gets bigger due to an extra filled electron shell/orbit/energy level. As potassium is further down the group than lithium, the potassium atom is larger than the lithium atom because its outer electron sits on a larger shell/orbit. This also means that potassium has more electrons arranged on more shells/orbits/energy levels and the outer electron is further and further from the nucleus. The additional full shells/orbits/energy levels of negative charged electrons on the potassium atom compared to the lithium atom have a greater shielding effect on the outer electron from most of the positive charge of the nucleus. Therefore the outer electron is less and less strongly held by the positive nucleus as the attractive force is decreased. This means the outer electron is more easily lost and potassium is more violently reactive when compared to lithium.

C2 Chemical Reactions (Pages 54–61)

1. Heat energy is given out to the surroundings
2. The reactants or H-H and Cl-Cl
3. Exothermic
4. Heat energy is needed to break bonds (1 mark); If the amount of energy released when making bonds is greater than the energy to break them then the overall reaction will generate heat and be exothermic (1 mark)
5. (a) Car exhaust fumes are pollutants and make the air unpleasant to breathe (1 mark); Carbon monoxide is toxic (1 mark)
   (b) Nitrogen monoxide + Carbon monoxide ⟶ Carbon dioxide + Nitrogen
6. 0.5g; it is a catalyst and not used up in the reaction
7. (a) A chemical that speeds a reaction up without being used itself
   (b) Points plotted correctly (1 mark); Labels on axes (1 mark); Curve drawn through points; time on horizontal and volume on vertical (1 mark)
   (c) Initially it is very fast (1 mark); then after 20 seconds, the amount of oxygen produced slows down as the decomposition slows down before all of the hydrogen peroxide is decomposed (1 mark)
8. Amount of product made per unit time or amount of reactant used up per unit time
9. Accept any two from: Changing the temperature; Changing concentration; Changing surface area; Using a catalyst; Changing pressure of a gas
10. Reduce temperature (less energy) (1 mark) and reduce concentration (less particles) (1 mark)
11. It can work in both directions (1 mark); Accept any suitable example (1 mark): Decomposition of ammonium chloride; Dehydration of copper sulfate crystals; Haber process
12. A should be ticked.

13. (a) As a catalyst, it will increase the rate of reaction
    *(b) If the reaction mixture is heated then the particles move more quickly so the particles collide with each other more often, with greater energy, and many more collisions are successful in a given time. This results in a faster rate of reaction. In a reaction where one or both reactants are in high concentrations or the pressure applied to the reactants is increased, the particles are packed closely together and collide with each other more often. This results in more successful collisions per second and results in a faster rate of reaction.
14. Butane has additional hydrogen-carbon and carbon-carbon bonds to break (1 mark); Also it will make more product so more bonds will be formed (1 mark); More energy will be generated in forming the additional molecules than with burning propane so the temperature rise will be greater (1 mark)
15. (a) The amount of carbon dioxide given off increases rapidly at first (1 mark) before levelling off when reaction has reached completion (1 mark)
    (b) A
    (c) More energy given to particles so successful collision occurs with greater frequency (1 mark) as reactants are used up quicker the amount of gas produced begins to level off in a shorter period of time (1 mark)
16. When reacting particles in chemical reactions collide with each other with sufficient energy to react.
17. (a) 13°C
    (b) Exothermic
18. (a) Given out
    (b) Exothermic (1 mark) because heat energy is given out when bonds are formed than when bonds are broken (1 mark)
19. (a) At first, the amount of gas produced increases rapidly (1 mark) before gradually levelling off as magnesium is used up (1 mark)
    (b) A
    (c) The amount of hydrogen released depends on the amount of magnesium used in the experiment (1 mark); The same amount of magnesium is used in all experiments, so the same amount of hydrogen is given off (1 mark)
*20. Increasing the temperature of the solution increases the rate of reaction as it results in more kinetic energy given to hydrochloric acid particles. The hydrochloric acid particles move faster, so there is a greater frequency of collisions with other reactant particles, As the collisions happen with greater energy they are more successful. Increasing the concentration of the hydrochloric acid increases the rate of reaction because it increases the number of acid particles so there are more particles available within the reaction environment. If there are more acid particles available to react, then there is a greater frequency of successful collisions with other reactant particles so the rate of reaction increases.

21.

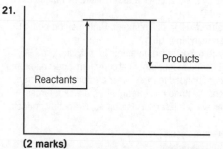

(2 marks)

C2 Quantitative Chemistry (Pages 62–67)

1. (a) 35.9 − 31.1 = 4.8g of titanium (1 mark)
       39.1 − 35.9 = 3.2g of oxygen (1 mark)
   (b) RFM TiO_2 = 48 + (16 × 2) = 80 (1 mark);
       Ti = $\frac{41}{48}$ = 0.85 (1 mark); Ti = TiO_2 so TiO_2 = 0.85 × 80
       = 68 (1 mark); % yield = $\left(\frac{63}{68}\right)$ × 100 = 92.6% (1 mark)
       (Accept +/− 0.5 due to rounding in calculation)

2. (a) Calculate maximum theoretical yield from mass of reactants (1 mark); Then divide actual yield by maximum theoretical yield and multiply by 100 (1 mark)

(b) RFM $Pb(NO_3)_2 = 207 + (14 \times 2) + [(16 \times 3) \times 2] = 331$
$PbSO_4 = 207 + 32 + (16 \times 4) = 303$ **(1 mark)**

$Pb(NO_3)_2 = \frac{329}{331} = 0.994$ **(1 mark)**

$Pb(NO_3)_2 = PbSO_4$ so amount of $= 0.994 \times 303 = 301.18$g
(1 mark)

% yield $= \left(\frac{293}{301.18}\right)$ g $\times 100 = 97.3\%$ **(1 mark)**

(ans to 3sf)

3. **(1 mark for each completed row)**

Aluminium chloride	$AlCl_3$	Al Cl	1 3	27 35.5	$1 \times 27 = 27$ $3 \times 35.5 = 106.5$	$27 + 106.5 = 133.5$
Copper oxide	CuO	Cu O	1 1	64 16	$1 \times 64 = 64$ $1 \times 16 = 16$	$64 + 16 = 80$
Copper sulfate	$CuSO_4$	Cu S O	1 1 4	64 32 16	$1 \times 64 = 64$ $1 \times 32 = 32$ $4 \times 16 = 64$	$64 + 32 + 64 = 160$
Calcium hydroxide	$Ca(OH)_2$	Ca O H	1 2 2	40 16 1	$1 \times 40 = 40$ $2 \times 16 = 32$ $2 \times 1 = 2$	$40 + 32 + 2 = 74$
Sodium carbonate	Na_2CO_3	Na C O	2 1 3	23 12 16	$2 \times 23 = 46$ $1 \times 12 = 12$ $3 \times 16 = 48$	$46 + 12 + 48 = 106$
Aluminium sulfate	$Al_2(SO_4)_3$	Al S O	2 3 12	27 32 16	$2 \times 27 = 54$ $3 \times 32 = 96$ $12 \times 16 = 192$	$54 + 96 + 192 = 342$

4. **(a)** $1 \times A_r$ of $X = 40 - 16 = 24$ $X = Mg$

(b) $2 \times A_r$ of $X = 62 - 16 = 46$ $A_r = \frac{46}{2} = 23$ $X = Na$

(c) $2 \times A_r$ of $X = 95 - 24 = 71$ $A_r = \frac{71}{2} = 35.5$ $X = Cl$

(d) $2 \times A_r$ of $X = 44 - 12 = 32$ $A_r = \frac{32}{2} = 16$ $X = O$

(e) $1 \times A_r$ of $X = 171 - 2 \times (16 + 1) = 171 - 34 = 137$ $X = Ba$

(f) $2 \times A_r$ of $X = 188 - (3 \times 16) = 188 - 48 = 140$

$A_r = \frac{140}{2} = 70$ $X = Ga$

5. **(a)** RFM $N_2H_4 = 2 \times 14 + 4 \times 1 = 32$; $2NH_3 = 2 \times (14 + 3 \times 1)$

$= 34$ **(1 mark)**; $\frac{170}{34} = 5$; $5 \times 32 = 160$g **(1 mark)**

(b) $\frac{135}{160} \times 100 = 84.4\%$

(c) There was a loss of product **(1 mark)**; The starting materials were impure **(1 mark)**; Other products were also produced **(1 mark)**

6. **(a)** RFM $CuO = 64 + 16 = 80$; $Cu = 64$ **(1 mark)**

80g of CuO so 78g $= \left(\frac{78}{80}\right) = 0.975$ **(1 mark)**

$2CuO = 2Cu$ this is the same as $1CuO = 1Cu$; so 0.975 $CuO = 0.975$ Cu or 0.975×64g $= 62.4$g **(1 mark)**

% yield $= \left(\frac{46}{62.4}\right)$ g $\times 100 = 73.7\%$ **(1 mark) (ans to 3sf)**

(b) Accept any one from: There was a loss of product; The starting materials were impure; Other products were also produced

7. **(a)** $CaCO_3$ $40 + 12 + (3 \times 16) = 100$; HCl $(1 + 35.5) = 36.5$ $CaCl_2$ $40 + (2 \times 35.5) = 111$; CO_2 $12 + (2 \times 16) = 44$; H_2O $(2 \times 1) + 16 = 18$ **(2 marks)**

(b) Conservation of mass means that no mass is lost or gained during a reaction and there is exactly the same number of atoms in the total products as there was in the total reactants

(c) 100g $CaCO_3$ reacts with 73g HCl (RFM 36.5, but 2 mols) 25g $CaCO_3$ reacts with $\frac{25}{100} \times 73$g of HCl $= 18.25$g

8. **Accept any two from:** Efficiency; To control temperature; To control pressure; To control chemical composition; To control flow rates

9. **(a)** RFM $NaHCO_3 = 23 + 1 + 12 + (16 \times 3) = 84$ $Na_2SO_4 = (23 \times 2) + 32 + (16 \times 4) = 142$ **(1 mark)**

84g of $NaHCO_3$ so 164g $= \left(\frac{164}{84}\right) = 1.95$ **(1 mark)**

$2NaHCO_3 = 1Na_2SO_4$ so 1.95 $NaHCO_3 = \left(\frac{1.95}{2}\right) Na_2SO_4$ or 0.975×142g $= 138.45$g **(1 mark)**

% yield $= \left(\frac{135}{138.45}\right)$ g $\times 100 = 97.5\%$ **(1 mark) (ans to 3sf)**

(Accept +/– 0.5 due to rounding in calculation)

(b) 84g of $NaHCO_3$ so 166g $= \left(\frac{166}{84}\right) = 1.98$ **(1 mark)**

$2NaHCO_3 = 1Na_2SO_4$ so 1.98 $NaHCO_3 = \left(\frac{1.98}{2}\right) Na_2SO_4$ or 0.99×142g $= 140.58$g **(1 mark)**

% yield $= \left(\frac{126}{140.58}\right)$ g $\times 100 = 89.6\%$ **(1 mark) (ans to 3sf)**

(Accept +/– 0.5 due to rounding in calculation)

10. RFM of $SiO_2 = 28 + (2 \times 16) = 60$. 60g of SiO_2 gives 28g of Si **(1 mark)** $\frac{60}{28}$ g of SiO_2 will make 1g of Si $= 2.14$g **(1 mark)**

11. $MgO + 2HCl \longrightarrow MgCl_2 + H_2O$

12. **(a)** RFM of $Fe_2O_3 = 112 + 48 = 160$; $= \frac{800}{160} = 5$; **(1 mark)** $Al = 2 \times 5 = 10$, mass $Al = 10 \times 27 = 270$g **(1 mark)**

(b) $1Fe_2O_3 = 2Fe$; $\frac{480}{160} = 3$; $Fe = 3 \times 2 = 6$; **(1 mark)** mass $Fe = 6 \times 56 = 336$g **(1 mark)**

(c) RFM: $Al = 27$; $Al_2O_3 = (27 \times 2) + (16 \times 3) = 102$ **(1 mark)** $2Al = 1Al_2O_3$ so $Al_2O_3 = \frac{408}{102} = 4$, $Al = 4 \times 2 = 8$ so mass $Al = 8 \times 27 = 216$g **(1 mark)**

13. Ammonium hydroxide $= \frac{140}{35} = 4$ **(1 mark)**; mass of ammonium nitrate $= 4 \times 80 = 320$g **(1 mark)**

P2 Static and Current Electricity (Pages 68–71)

1. **(a)** Any metal **(b)** Most non-metals **(c)** Conductors allow electricity to flow, insulators do not

2. **(a)** Friction/rubbing with another insulator **(b)** Static electricity

3. **(a)** Electrons **(1 mark)** go from balloon to jumper **(1 mark)** **(b) (i)** Positive **(ii)** Fewer electrons/less negative charge on balloon

4. **(a)** Repels/moves away **(b)** Both (rods) have the same charge **(1 mark)** same charges repel **(1 mark)**

5. Perspex rod has opposite charge **(1 mark)** to ebonite rod **(1 mark)** opposite charges attract **(1 mark)**

6. Shoes rub on carpet **(1 mark)** shoes/Salma gains charge **(1 mark)** charge flows to (metal) radiator **(1 mark)**

7. **(a)** Electrons flow/move **(1 mark)** from one object to another **(1 mark)**

(b)

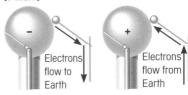

Electrons flow to Earth

Electrons flow from Earth

(1 mark)   **(1 mark)**

8. **(a)-(b) Accept any two from:** Laser printer; Photocopier; Xerox copier; Paint sprayer; Insecticide sprayer; Computer memory; Removal of smoke from factory chimneys; Air ionisers; Defibrillators

9. **(a)** Fuel gains electrons (from pipe)/pipe loses electrons (to fuel) **(1 mark)**, so the pipe becomes positively charged, the fuel becomes negatively charged **(1 mark)**, this results in a potential difference/voltage, between the pipe and the fuel **(1 mark)**, this could lead to a discharge/spark/explosion **(1 mark)**

(b) Tank can be earthed/tanker and plane can be linked with (copper) conductor

10. **(a)** 20C **(b)** 45C **(c)** 0.75×80 **(1 mark)** $= 60$C **(1 mark)**

11. **(a)** (Atmospheric) discharge **(1 mark)** of static electricity **(1 mark)** **(b)** Separation of charges builds up **(1 mark)**; Cloud induces positive charge on ground **(1 mark)**; Potential difference between ground and cloud **(1 mark)**; Electrons jump from cloud to ground **(1 mark)**

*12. The conductor is the tallest, positively charged object on the building. A (thunder) cloud induces a positive charge on the top of the conductor. The conductor provides an easier path for charges to flow because it is made of copper and copper has a low electrical resistance. So the conductor provides a path for the charges to flow to Earth, rather than through the building.

*13. Paint is forced through a nozzle. This breaks it in to very small droplets. The small drops of paint are made to be electrically charged, thereby repelling each other; this causes them to spread themselves evenly as they exit the spray nozzle. The object being painted is charged oppositely or grounded. The paint is then attracted to the object giving a more even coat than wet spray painting.

14. $\dfrac{3.2 \times 10^{-2}}{0.014}$ **(1 mark)** = 2.3s **(1 mark)**

15. $\dfrac{6.72 \times 10^{-4}}{23.5}$ **(1 mark)** = 2.86×10^{-5}A **(1 mark)**

P2 Controlling and Using Electric Current (Pages 72–78)

1. **(a)**

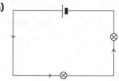

(1 mark for correct symbols, 1 mark for correct positions)

(b)

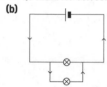

(1 mark for correct symbols, 1 mark for correct positions)

2.

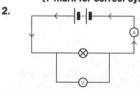

(a) (1 mark for correct symbol, 1 mark for correct position - ammeter can be anywhere in the line of the circuit)
(b) (1 mark for correct symbol, 1 mark for correct position)

3. **(a)** 0.2A **(b)** 0.4A
4. **(a)** Dimmer/less bright
    (b) Brighter
    (c) **(i)** Number of cells increase **(1 mark)**, brightness increases **(1 mark)**
        (ii) Voltage increases **(1 mark)**, current increases **(1 mark)**
5. **(a)** **(i)** How hard it is for current to flow
        (ii) Ohms, Ω
    (b) Reduces/gets smaller
    (c) Variable resistor
6. **(a)**

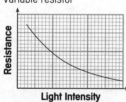

(1 mark for each axis labelled correctly)
    (b) As light intensity/light level increases **(1 mark)** resistance decreases **(1 mark)**
    (c) **Accept any one from:** Automatic light detector; Control exposure in camera; In a circuit to switch on/off a light, etc.
7. **(a)**

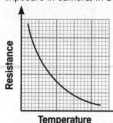

(1 mark for each axis labelled correctly, 1 mark for curve as shown)

(b) The resistance of a light bulb increases as temperature increases **(1 mark)**, the resistance of a thermistor decreases as temperature increases **(1 mark)**, this is similar to the way the resistance of an LDR changes/varies or the graph looks the same. But its resistance changes/varies with light (intensity), not temperature **(1 mark)**

8. **(a)** **(i)** Current **(ii)** Resistance **(any order)**
    (b) 0.6×10 **(1 mark)** = 6V **(1 mark)**
9. **(a)** **(i)** 3V **(ii)** 6Ω **(iii)** 0.5A **(iv)** 1V **(v)** 2V
    (b) **(i)** 6V **(ii)** 8Ω **(iii)** 0.75A **(iv)** 1.5V **(v)** 4.5V
    (c) **(i)** 6V **(ii)** 10Ω **(iii)** 0.6A **(iv)** 1.2V **(v)** 4.8V
    ((a)–(c) 5 correct = 3 marks; 3–4 correct = 2 marks; 1–2 correct = 1 mark)

10. **(a)**

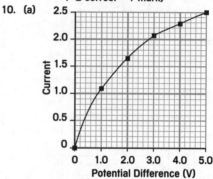

Current (A) on y-axis **(1 mark)**; Potential difference(V) on x-axis **(1 mark)**; Correct plotting **(1 mark)**; Smooth curve **(1 mark)**

    (b) **(i)** Curve **(1 mark)** as p.d. increases current increases **(1 mark)** at a smaller rate/current tends to maximum **(1 mark)** as filament heats up **(1 mark)**
        (ii) Resistance increases **(1 mark)** as the temperature of the bulb increases **(1 mark)**

11. **(a)** A **(b)** C **(c)** B
12. **Accept any one from:** Hairdryer; Immersion heater; Kettle; Toaster; Light bulb, etc.
13. Electrical **(1 mark)** to thermal/heat **(1 mark)**
14. **(a)** 230×5 **(1 mark)** = 1150W **(1 mark)**
    (b) **(i)** 1150J
        (ii) 1150×60 **(1 mark)** = 69 000J **(1 mark)**
*15. Set up a circuit with an ammeter in series with an LDR. A voltmeter must be connected in parallel with the LDR. With the room blacked out or darkened, a variable brightness lamp is directed at the LDR and the light intensity varied. For each setting of the lamp, the potential difference and current are recorded. Finally, plot a graph of current against potential difference.
16. **(a)** **(i)** 0.01A **(ii)** (Much) bigger **(1 mark)** 74 times bigger **(1 mark)**
    (b) **(i)** R (lamp): $\dfrac{3.4}{0.74}$ **(1 mark)** = 4.6Ω **(1 mark)**
        (ii) R(voltmeter): $\dfrac{3.4}{0.01}$ **(1 mark)** = 340Ω **(1 mark)**
17. **(a)** 3.4J **(b)** 15×3.4 **(1 mark)** = 51J **(1 mark)**
18. $\dfrac{30}{230}$ **(1 mark)** = 0.13A **(1 mark)**
19. $\dfrac{90}{4.7}$ **(1 mark)** = 19V **(1 mark)**
20. **(a)** It gets hot/becomes heated
    (b) Electrons collide **(1 mark)** with ions **(1 mark)** in lattice **(1 mark)**; Energy is transferred from electrons to ions **(1 mark)**
21. **(a)** $V = \dfrac{E}{Q}$ **(1 mark)** $E = I \times \dfrac{E}{Q} \times t$ **(1 mark)** $Q = I \times t$ **(1 mark)**
    (b) **(i)** $\dfrac{25\,000}{1100}$ = 22.7 = 23s (to 2sf)
        (ii) $\dfrac{1100}{240}$ **(1 mark)** = 4.6A = **(1 mark)**

P2 Motion and Forces (Pages 79–84)

1. C **should be ticked.**

2. **(a) (i)** $\frac{25}{5}$ **(1 mark)** = 5m/s **(1 mark) (ii)** $\frac{25}{20}$ **(1 mark)**

   1.25m/s **(1 mark)**

   (b) 50m
   (c) Walks at steady speed (for 5s) **(1 mark)**, stops (for 5s)
   (1 mark), then walks back at slower speed (for 2Os) **(1 mark)**

3. $\frac{(15-0)}{30}$ **(1 mark)** = 0.5m/s² **(1 mark)**

4. **(a)** D **(b)** A **(c)** B and C **(d)** A

5. $\frac{150}{5}$ **(1 mark)** = 30m/s² **(1 mark)**

6. **(a)** Driving force is bigger than the resistive force
   (b) Forces are equal
   (c) Driving force is less than the resistive force

7. **(a)**

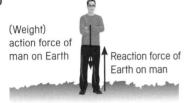

(Weight)
action force of
man on Earth   Reaction force of
Earth on man

**(1 mark for reaction force of man on Earth up arrow and
1 mark for the weight down arrow. 1 mark for arrows being
the same length.)**

   (b) Upthrust (due to the displacement
   of air surrounding balloon)

**(1 mark for up arrow labelled
upthrust, 1 mark for down
arrow labelled weight, 1 mark
for up arrow longer than down
arrow, credit to be given if
downward force air resistance
is labelled)**

Weight

8. **(a)** 450N **(b)** 9000N
9. 800 × 1.5 **(1 mark)** = 1200N **(1 mark)**
10. **(a)** 0.4m/s² **(b) (i)** 1000N **(ii)** 0.5m/s²
11. D **should be ticked.**
12. **(a) (i)** Accelerates; because of weight/gravity
   (ii) Acceleration less because of air resistance
   (iii) Acceleration even less as air resistance increases
   (iv) No acceleration; weight = air resistance; reaches
   terminal velocity
   (b) Parachute opens
   (c) (i) Speed decreases since air resistance bigger
   (ii) Speed further decreases so air resistance less
   (iii) Steady speed/no acceleration; weight = air resistance;
   reaches terminal velocity
   (iv) Speed zero – lands on ground
*13. The runway needs to be raised until the trolley moves at
   constant speed or velocity. This means there is no (zero)
   acceleration, which implies no (zero) resultant force acting on
   the trolley. Since the runway has friction, raising the slope
   eliminates the need to take friction into account. Any extra force
   on the trolley will then be the accelerating force. Raising the
   slope would not be necessary if the runway was smooth/friction
   free (but that is unlikely).

14. $v = \frac{90 \times 1000}{3600} = 25$m/s **(1 mark)** $u = v - a \times t$ **(1 mark)**

   25 − 2 × 5 **(1 mark)** = 15m/s **(1 mark)**

15. $m = F/a = \frac{20000}{0.8} = 25000$kg

16. **(a)** 3000N
   (b) Resultant = 1000N **(1 mark)** 1m/s² **(1 mark)**
   (c) v = 30 + 1 × 20 **(1 mark)** = 50m/s **(1 mark)**

17. **(a)** $\frac{25}{(5 \times 60)}$ **(1 mark)** = 0.083m/s² **(1 mark)**

   (b) 25 × 5 × 60 **(1 mark)** = 7500m **(1 mark)**

(c) 0.5 × 300 × 25 + 7500 + 0.5 × 20 × 60 × 25 **(1 mark)**
= 26 250m **(1 mark)**

(d) $\frac{25}{(20 \times 60)}$ **(1 mark)** = 0.021m/s² **(1 mark)**

(e) $\frac{26\,250}{(30 \times 60)}$ **(1 mark)** = 14.6m/s **(1 mark)**

P2 Momentum, Energy, Work and Power (Pages 85–90)

1. **(a)** Thinking distance **(b)** Braking distance
2. C **should be ticked.**
3. **(a)** Time from seeing child **(1 mark)** to applying brakes **(1 mark)**
   (b) (i)-(ii) Accept any two from: Drinking alcohol; Taking drugs;
   Being distracted; Using mobile
4. B **Should be ticked.**
5. **(a)-(b) In any order:** Mass, Velocity
6. **(a)** 1000 × 20 **(1 mark)** = 20 000kg m/s **(1 mark)**
   (b) −20 000kg m/s
7. Total mass 340kg **(1 mark)** $\frac{8500}{340}$ **(1 mark)** = 25m/s **(1 mark)**
8. **(a)** (Total) momentum before collision = (Total) momentum after
   collision **(b) (i)** 800 × 20 + 800 × 30 **(1 mark)** 40 000kg m/s
   (1 mark) (ii) 40 000kg m/s
9. 150 × 1500 **(1 mark)** = 225 000J **(1 mark)**
10. **(a)** 50 × 1.8 **(1 mark)** = 90J **(1 mark) (b)** 90J **(c)** Energy
   transferred = work done
11. **(a)** 50 000 × 30 **(1 mark)** = 1 500 000J **(1 mark)**
   (b) $\frac{1\,500\,000}{20}$ **(1 mark)** 75 000W/75kW **(1 mark)**
12. **(a)** Energy gained by lifting object above ground/m × g × h with
   m, g, h explained **(b) (i)-(ii) Accept any answer where the object
   is above ground, e.g.** Diver on board; Book on bookshelf, etc.
13. 50 × 10 × 5 **(1 mark)** = 2500J **(1 mark)**
14. **(a)** 0.4 × 10 × 8 **(1 mark)** = 32J **(1 mark) (b)** Transfers to KE
15. **(a)-(b) Accept any two examples where object is moving, e.g.**
   Moving car; Running man, etc.
16. 0.5 × 2000 × 20² **(1 mark)** = 400 000J **(1 mark)**
17. **(a)** (iv) **(b)** (iii) **(c)** (i) **(d)** (ii)
*18. Attach a newton meter to the block or attach a mass holder
   by string (over a pulley) to the block. Pull the block along the
   surface or place masses on the holder to make the block move.
   Make sure the block moves steadily. Record the force (in
   newtons). Repeat this to get an average force. Change the surface
   to make it rougher or smoother and repeat the experiment.
19. Air bags increase time of stopping **(1 mark)** rate of change of
   momentum less **(1 mark)** force acting less **(1 mark)**
20. **(a)** 20m/s **(b)** 20m **(c)** 4s **(d)** 60m
21. **(a)** 10⁴ × 10 × 120 **(1 mark)** = 1.2 × 10⁷ J/12MJ **(1 mark)**
   (b) $\frac{1.2 \times 10^{7}}{200}$ **(1 mark)** = 60 000W/60kW **(1 mark)**
22. D **should be ticked.**
23. Change in momentum = F × t **(1 mark)** 2000 × 0.45 **(1 mark)**
   = 900 **(1 mark)** kg m/s **(1 mark)**
24. **(a)** 750 × 20 − 750 × 5 **(1 mark)** = 11 250kg m/s **(1 mark)**
   (b) Rate of change of momentum = $\frac{11\,250}{5}$ **(1 mark)** force
   = 2250N **(1 mark)**
25. **(a)** Work done = KE
   (b) WD = F × d **(1 mark)** KE = 0.5 × m × v² **(1 mark)**
   Fd = 0.5mv² **(1 mark)** F and m are constant, therefore d
   proportional to v² **(1 mark)**
   (c) $\frac{0.5 \times 5000 \times 25^{2}}{10\,000}$ **(1 mark)** = 156m **(1 mark)**
*26. The energy to stop the vehicle is equal to its kinetic energy.
   The energy is the force times the distance to stop the car. Connor
   is right that there is more energy if it goes faster, since more
   means greater kinetic energy. Habiba is right that energy is not
   proportional to the velocity, since kinetic energy is proportional to
   the square of the velocity, so that energy or the stopping distance
   is also proportional to the square of the velocity. But Habiba says
   the stopping distance is 'much more' (at greater speeds) which
   isn't clear.

P2 Nuclear Fission and Nuclear Fusion (Pages 91–96)

1. **(a)** Proton **(b)** Neutron **(c)** Electron
2. **(a)** (Element with) same number of protons **(1 mark)**, different number of neutrons **(1 mark) (b) (i)** 27, 27 **(ii)** 33, 32 **(iii)** 27, 27 **(1 mark for each correct row)**
3. A = mass number/number or protons + neutrons; Z = atomic number/number of protons/electrons
4. $^{60}_{27}Co$ $^{59}_{27}Co$
5. (Unstable) nucleus that splits/disintegrates/emits radiation
6. **(a)** (i), (iii), (vii) **(b)** (i), (v), (vi) **(c)** (i), (ii), (iv)
7. **(a)** Beta and gamma **(b)** Aluminium or lead **(c)** Gamma
8. **(a) Accept any three from:** Radiation collides with atoms; Atoms lose electron/s; Atoms become charged; Charged atoms are called ions
   (b) Alpha
9. Nuclear fission: fission-splitting **(1 mark)** of large/heavy nucleus **(1 mark)**; Nuclear fusion: Fusion-joining **(1 mark)** of light nuclei **(1 mark)**
10.
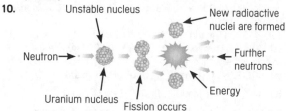

Unstable nucleus

New radioactive nuclei are formed

Neutron→

Further neutrons

Energy

Uranium nucleus   Fission occurs

(7 correct = 4 marks; 5–6 correct = 3 marks; 3–4 correct = 2 marks; 1–2 correct = 1 mark)
11. **(a)** Nuclear reactor **(b)** Atomic bomb **(c) (i)-(ii)** Control rods; Moderator
12. Fission occurs in the nuclear reactor **(1 mark)**, this produces heat/thermal energy **(1 mark)**; this energy is used to heat water in the heat exchanger, which produces steam that then drives the turbines/makes the turbines rotate **(1 mark)**; the turbines are connected to the generator that turns to produce electricity **(1 mark)**
13. Cannot be predicted when radiation will be emitted/radiation is not emitted at constant intervals of time
14. **(a)** (Two) smaller nuclei **(1 mark)**, (More) neutrons **(1 mark)**, Energy **(1 mark) (b)** Radioactive **(c)** It must be stored/carefully disposed of
15. **(a)** Chain reaction **(b)** Neutron splits nucleus **(1 mark)**; (More) neutrons produced **(1 mark)**; Neutrons split more nuclei **(1 mark)**
16. Controlled: thermal energy used to make steam **(1 mark)** in nuclear reactor **(1 mark)**; Uncontrolled: enormous/huge amount of energy released **(1 mark)** in atomic bomb **(1 mark)**
17. Two or more light/small nuclei **(1 mark)** join/combine to form a heavy nuclei **(1 mark)** with the release of energy **(1 mark)**
18. **(a)** High temperature **(1 mark)** nuclei driven **(1 mark)** to overcome electrostatic repulsion **(1 mark)**
    (b) High pressure **(1 mark)** high density of nuclei **(1 mark)** ensures collisions **(1 mark)**
    (c) In stars
19.

Deuterium

Helium

Energy

Neutron

Tritium   Fusion occurs

(6 correct = 3 marks; 4–5 correct = 2 marks; 2–3 correct = 1 mark)
20. **(a)** Temperature of fuel **(1 mark)** must be heated to 100 million °C/6 times hotter than the Sun **(1 mark)**
    (b) Pressure of fuel **(1 mark)** needs to be extremely high - this is difficult to achieve **(1 mark)**
    (c) Confinement of fuel **(1 mark)**, no ordinary vessel can be used (at such high temperatures and pressures) **(1 mark)**

*21. The theory of cold fusion is nuclear fusion which occurs at room temperature. However, fusion needs (very) high temperatures in order to take place because there is electrostatic repulsion between protons. As the experiment has not been reproduced convincingly by scientists, the theory of cold fusion is not generally accepted at the moment.

P2 Advantages and Disadvantages of Using Radioactive Materials (Pages 97–101)

1. C **should be ticked**.
2. **(a)** Medical/food
   (b) Radon gas
3. **(a)-(b) Accept any two from:** Smoke alarm; Irradiating food; Sterilising equipment; Monitoring thickness; Diagnosis of cancer; Treatment of cancer; Dating of old fossils, etc.
4. **(a)** Time taken **(1 mark)** for half **(1 mark)** of the nuclei to change/decay **(1 mark)**
   (b) (i) 800Bq **(ii)** 200Bq **(c)** 3 p.m.
5. **(a)** 8 days
   ***(b)** Yes the scientists were right because the half-life of caesium is 30 years. So after four months it will still be very active and not much of it will have decayed. The half-life of iodine is much shorter than caesium at only 8 days (or the value quoted in (a)). After four months almost all or very nearly all of the iodine will have decayed.
6. **(a)** 2 original, one half-life 460 years; 3 original, two half-lives 920 years; $\frac{1}{8}$ original, three half-lives **(1 mark)** eight = 1380 years **(1 mark)**
   (b) Yes. Doesn't need replacing; still effective after a long time/many years
7. Can damage cells/cause cancer **(1 mark)**; Can cause mutations (in future generations) **(1 mark)**
8. **(a)** Alpha **(1 mark)** stopped by skin/can't penetrate body **(1 mark) (b)** Beta and gamma **(1 mark)** less likely to be absorbed by cells **(1 mark)**
9. **(a)** Protective clothing/not being too near **(b)** Limit exposure time/use short half-life source
10. **(a)** (Hands of) watches/aircraft instruments **(b)** Injuries/deaths reported
11. Advantages: **Accept any two from:** No air pollutants; Waste is small; Fuel costs low; Jobs created
    Disadvantages: **Accept any two from:** Risk of major accident; Waste dangerous; Transport/storage of waste difficult; Construction/maintenance costs high; Security a problem; A lot of land used; Visual pollution; Habitats destroyed; Increase in traffic causing noise/air pollution
12. **(a)** High level; medium level; low level **(b) (i)** Low level **(ii)** Protective clothing/laboratory equipment
13. **(a)** 50 years **(b)** One sixty-fourth $(\frac{1}{2})^6$
14. **(a)** Alpha absorbed by smoke but beta and gamma would not be **(1 mark)**; Alpha stopped by plastic case (so safe to use) **(1 mark)**
    (b) The alpha radiation ionises the air particles producing ions **(1 mark)**, which are attracted to the electrodes causing a current to flow **(1 mark)**; When there is a fire, alpha particles are absorbed by the smoke particles **(1 mark)**; This results in less ionisation and a smaller current to flow which activates the alarm/makes the alarm sound **(1 mark)**
15. **(a)** About 2 half-lives **(1 mark)** age about 2 × 5730 = 11460 years **(1 mark) (b) (i)** Because activity measured 450Bq not 435Bq **(ii)** Actual age should be (a bit) less
16. **(a)** Spent fuel rods **(1 mark)** short term: store in pool of liquid (to absorb radiation) **(1 mark)**; Long term: bury (deep) underground **(1 mark)** in (tightly) sealed containers **(1 mark)**
    (b) (i) Less radioactive **(ii)** Stored in drums/containers **(1 mark)** above ground **(1 mark)** and monitored **(1 mark)**

7. A catalyst is used to speed up the decomposition of hydrogen peroxide which can be shown in the symbol equation:

$$2H_2O_{2(aq)} \longrightarrow O_{2(g)} + 2H_2O_{(l)}$$

0.5g of catalyst was added to a flask containing 100cm³ of hydrogen peroxide at 20°C.
A gas was released. This gas was collected and its volume recorded every 10 seconds. The table shows the results.

Time (sec)	0	10	20	30	40	50	60	70	80	90
Volume of Gas (cm³)	0	15	28	39	46	51	56	59	59	59

(a) What is a **catalyst**? (1)

_____

(b) Plot a graph of the results on the grid below. (3)

(c) Describe how the rate of decomposition of the hydrogen peroxide changes during the reaction. (2)

....

....

....

8. How can the rate of a chemical reaction be defined? (1)

....

9. List **two** ways in which you can change the rate of a chemical reaction. (2)

....

....

....

10. How could you use temperature and concentration to slow down the rate of a chemical reaction? (2)

....

....

11. What does it mean for a chemical reaction to be **reversible**? Give a suitable example. (2)

....

....

....

12. Chemical reactions can happen at different speeds, for example, some can be very fast and some can be very slow. Tick the option below that shows the fastest chemical reaction. (1)

A ☐ Firework exploding

B ☐ Baking a cake

C ☐ Iron gate rusting

D ☐ Frying an egg

(Total: .... / 23)

13. Ammonia is manufactured by the Haber process, in which nitrogen and hydrogen react according to the equation:

$N_2 + 3H_2 \rightleftharpoons 2NH_3$

(a) Why is iron used in the Haber process and what effect does it have? (1)

....

*(b) Explain in terms of frequency of collision of particles how increasing temperature, pressure and concentration affect this chemical reaction. (6)

....

....

....

....

....

....

....

....

....

....

....

14. Explain why burning 1 molecule of butane completely in air is more exothermic than burning 1 molecule of propane completely in air. (3)

....

....

....

....

continued...

15. The word equation below shows the reaction between calcium carbonate and dilute hydrochloric acid.

Calcium carbonate + Hydrochloric acid ⟶ Calcium chloride + Water + Carbon dioxide

The rate of the chemical reaction can be studied by measuring the amount of carbon dioxide gas produced.

The graph below shows the results of four experiments A, B, C and D. For each of the experiments, only the temperature of the acid was changed.

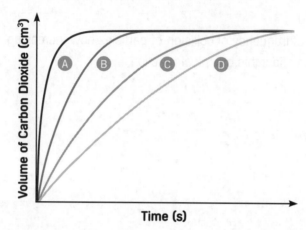

(a) In terms of the carbon dioxide gas produced, describe, as fully as you can, the rate of the reaction as shown by graph B. (2)

_____

_____

_____

(b) Which graph shows the results of the experiment with the acid at the highest temperature? (1)

_____

(c) Using collision theory, explain your answer to part **(b)**. (2)

_____

_____

_____

16. What is meant by collision theory? (1)

_____

continued...

17. Camping stoves use a hydrocarbon gas called propane as a fuel. Propane has the formula C_3H_8. In an experiment, 1g of propane was used to heat $1000cm^3$ of water. The temperature of the water rose from $20^{\circ}C$ to $33^{\circ}C$.

(a) By how much did the temperature of the water rise? (1)

....

(b) Is the burning of this gas **endothermic** or **exothermic**? (1)

....

18. The following energy diagram represents the energies involved for the reaction between sodium hydroxide and hydrochloric acid.

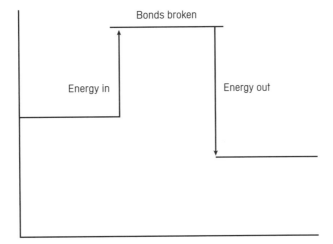

Bonds broken

Energy in

Energy out

(a) Is heat given out or taken in during the chemical reaction? (1)

....

(b) What type of chemical reaction is the diagram showing? Explain your answer. (2)

....

....

....

continued...

19. The word equation below shows the reaction between magnesium and excess dilute hydrochloric acid.

Magnesium + Hydrochloric acid ⟶ Magnesium chloride + Hydrogen

The rate of the chemical reaction can be studied by measuring the amount of hydrogen gas produced.

The graph below shows the results of three experiments A, B and C. For each of the experiments, only the concentration of the acid was changed.

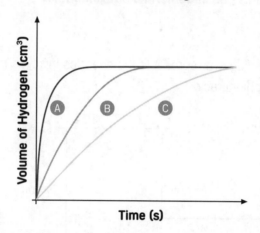

(a) In terms of hydrogen gas produced, describe, as fully as you can, the rate of reaction as shown by graph A. (2)

(b) Which graph shows the results of the experiment with the acid at the highest concentration? (1)

(c) Explain your answer to **(b)** and why the total volume of gas given off was the same, regardless of the concentration of the acid. (2)

continued...

*20. Explain the effect of increasing the temperature and concentration of the hydrochloric acid on the rate of the reaction in question 19 in terms of the kinetic energy of the reacting particles and the frequency of the collisions. (6)

21. When ammonium chloride is dissolved in water, it is accompanied by a temperature drop. In the space below, draw an energy diagram that would show the energy changes occurring as the ammonium chloride dissolves. (2)

(Total: .... / 34)

Questions labelled with an asterisk (*) are ones where the quality of your written communication will be assessed – you should take particular care with your spelling, punctuation and grammar, as well as the clarity of expression, on these questions.

1. A student heated strongly a known mass of titanium so that all the titanium combined with oxygen from the air. The following results were obtained.

   Mass of container + titanium   = 35.9g

   Mass of empty container   = 31.1g

   Mass of container + contents after heating = 39.1g

   (Relative atomic mass: Ti = 48, O = 16)

   (a) Calculate the mass of titanium and of oxygen combining in the experiment. (2)

   ....

   ....

   ....

   (b) In an experiment 63g of titanium dioxide, TiO_2 was obtained when 41g of titanium, Ti was reacted with oxygen. What is the percentage yield of this reaction? (4)

   ....

   ....

   ....

   ....

2. **(a)** Describe how you would work out a chemical yield. (2)

   ....

   ....

   ....

   (b) 293g of lead sulfate was obtained from the reaction of 329g lead nitrate and sulfuric acid. What is the percentage yield of the reaction? (Relative atomic mass: Pb = 207, O = 16, S = 32, N = 14) (4)

   $$Pb(NO_3)_2(aq) + H_2SO_4(aq) \longrightarrow PbSO_4(s) + 2HNO_3(aq)$$

   ....

   ....

   ....

3. Using the information in the table below, calculate the relative formula mass of the listed compounds. (6)

Hydrogen, H($A_r = 1$)	Oxygen, O($A_r = 16$)	Sodium, Na($A_r = 23$)	Carbon, C($A_r = 12$)
Aluminium, Al ($A_r = 27$)	Chlorine, Cl($A_r = 35.5$)	Calcium, Ca($A_r = 40$)	
Nitrogen, N($A_r = 14$)	Copper, Cu($A_r = 64$)	Sulfur, S($A_r = 32$)	

The first one has been done for you. (Remember each capital letter **not** the small letter is a different element.)

Compound	Formula	Elements	Number of each Element	Relative Atomic Mass, A_r	Total for each Element	Total Mass of Compound, RFM
Water	H_2O	H	2	1	$1 \times 2 = 2$	$2 + 16 = 18$
		O	1	16	$16 \times 1 = 16$	
Aluminium chloride	$AlCl_3$					
Copper oxide	CuO					
Copper sulfate	$CuSO_4$					
Calcium hydroxide	$Ca(OH)_2$					
Sodium carbonate	Na_2CO_3					
Aluminium sulfate	$Al_2(SO_4)_3$					

4. In the following compounds, **X** is an unknown element. The relative formula mass of the compound is given in brackets (Relative atomic mass: C = 12, Mg = 24, H = 1, O = 16). Work out which element **X** represents in each example (use the periodic table to help you).

   (a) XO   (40) .... (1)

   (b) X_2O (62) .... (1)

   (c) MgX_2 (95) .... (1)

   (d) CX_2 (44) .... (1)

   (e) $X(OH)_2$ (171) .... (1)

   (f) X_2O_3 (188) .... (1)

5. Hydrazine (N_2H_4) can be made from the reaction between ammonia (NH_3) and excess sodium chlorate, NaOCl. The equation for the reaction is:

   $$2NH_3 + NaOCl \longrightarrow N_2H_4 + NaCl + H_2O$$

   (Relative atomic mass: O = 16, H = 1, N = 14, Na = 23, Cl = 35.5)

   (a) Calculate the maximum theoretical mass of hydrazine that can be made by reacting 170g of ammonia with sodium chlorate.   (2)

   ....

   ....

   ....

   (b) In the reaction, only 135g of hydrazine was produced. Calculate the percentage yield.   (1)

   ....

   ....

   ....

   (c) Give **three** reasons why there was less than the maximum theoretical yield of hydrazine produced.   (3)

   ....

   ....

   ....

   ....

6. In an experiment, only 46g of copper was obtained from 78g of copper oxide.
(Relative atomic mass: Cu = 64, C = 12, O = 16)

The equation for this reaction is $2CuO_{(s)} + C_{(s)} \longrightarrow 2Cu_{(s)} + CO_{2(g)}$

(a) Calculate the percentage yield of copper from copper oxide. (4)

(b) Suggest a reason why the yield was less than 100%. (1)

(Total: _____ **/ 35)**

Higher Tier

7. Calcium carbonate and hydrochloric acid react together to produce calcium chloride, carbon dioxide and water. The equation for this reaction is:

$CaCO_{3(s)} + 2HCl_{(g)} \longrightarrow CaCl_{2(aq)} + CO_{2(g)} + H_2O_{(l)}$

(a) Work out the relative formula mass, M_r, for each of the reactants and products shown in the equation. (Relative atomic mass: Ca = 40, C = 12, O = 16, H = 1, Cl = 35.5) (2)

(b) Explain why the total masses of the reactants and the products are the same. (1)

(c) What mass of hydrochloric acid would be needed to react fully with 25g of calcium carbonate? (1)

continued...

8. Give **two** reasons why a large-scale chemical process would use a continuous process. (2)

9. (a) What is the percentage yield of sodium sulfate in the reaction of sodium hydrogencarbonate and sulfuric acid if 135g of sodium sulfate was obtained from 164g of sodium hydrogencarbonate? Use the following equation to help you. (4)

$$2NaHCO_{3(s)} + H_2SO_{4(aq)} \longrightarrow Na_2SO_{4(aq)} + 2CO_{2(g)} + 2H_2O_{(l)}$$

(Relative atomic masses: Na = 23, H = 1, C = 12, O = 16, S = 32)

(b) In another reaction only 126g of sodium sulfate was produced when reacted with 166g of sodium hydrogen carbonate. What was the percentage yield of this reaction? (3)

10. Silicon is an important element used in the electronics industry. It can be made by heating a mixture of silicon dioxide with magnesium. The equation for this reaction is:

$$SiO_{2(s)} + 2Mg_{(s)} \longrightarrow 2MgO_{(s)} + Si_{(s)}$$

Calculate the mass of silicon dioxide needed to make 1g of silicon.
(Relative atomic mass: O = 16, Si = 28) (2)

11. A mixture of magnesium oxide and silicon is added to a beaker containing hydrochloric acid. The silicon is then filtered from solution. The reaction between magnesium oxide and hydrochloric acid forms magnesium chloride, $MgCl_2$ solution and water. Write a balanced symbol equation for this reaction. (2)

continued...

12. Iron is made when aluminium reacts with iron oxide. It can be shown in the following balanced symbol equation. (Relative atomic mass: Fe = 56, Al = 27, O = 16)

$$Fe_2O_3(s) + 2Al(s) \longrightarrow 2Fe(s) + Al_2O_3(s)$$

(a) What is the mass of aluminium needed to react with 800g of iron oxide? (2)

(b) What mass of iron is produced from 480g of iron oxide? (2)

(c) How much aluminium will be needed if 408g of aluminium oxide is produced? (2)

13. Ammonium nitrate can be produced from the reaction between ammonium hydroxide and nitric acid. (Relative atomic mass: N = 14, H = 1, O = 16)

$$NH_4OH(aq) + HNO_3(aq) \longrightarrow NH_4NO_3(aq) + H_2O(l)$$

How much ammonium nitrate is produced when 140g of ammonium hydroxide is reacted with nitric acid? (2)

(Total: .... / 25)

Questions labelled with an asterisk (*) are ones where the quality of your written communication will be assessed – you should take particular care with your spelling, punctuation and grammar, as well as the clarity of expression, on these questions.

1. **(a)** Give an example of an electrical **conductor**. (1)

   (b) Give an example of an electrical **insulator**. (1)

   (c) In terms of the flow of electricity, what is the difference between a conductor and an insulator? (1)

2. It is possible for an insulator to gain an electrical charge.

   (a) How can this be done? (1)

   (b) Complete this sentence.

   The insulator is then said to be charged with .... (1)

3. Sven rubs a balloon on his jumper, charging it.

   (a) His jumper gains a negative charge. Explain how. (2)

   (b) (i) What charge does the balloon gain? (1)

   (ii) Explain your answer. (1)

4. Two ebonite rods are rubbed with fur. One of these rods is suspended from a string.

   (a) What will happen to the suspended rod if the other rod is moved close to it? (1)

   (b) Explain your answer. (2)

5. Sean brings a charged ebonite rod near to a suspended and charged Perspex rod. He notices that the suspended rod moves towards the other rod. How can he explain this observation? (3)

6. Salma was in her classroom, which has a nylon carpet. She found that walking over the carpet and then touching the metal radiator gave her an electric shock. Explain why this happened. (3)

7. Earthing allows excess charge to be removed from an object.

    (a) Explain this in terms of the movement of electrons. (2)

    (b) The diagrams below show the dome of a Van de Graaf generator. (2)

    The dome on the left is negatively charged. A small sphere connected to earth touches the dome.

    (i) Draw arrows to show what happens to the flow of electrons.

    (ii) Do the same to the diagram on the right where the dome is positively charged.

8. Give the names of **two** examples of everyday products that make use of static electricity.

    (a) .... (1)

    (b) .... (1)

9. During the refuelling of planes, great care must be taken to avoid dangerous electrical discharges.

    (a) How could a discharge occur? (4)

(b) Give **one** way in which this could be prevented. (1)

10. Calculate the charge, in coulombs, that flows when:

(a) a current of 2A flows for 10s (1)

(b) a current of 1.5A flows for 30s (1)

(c) a current of 0.75A flows for 1 minute 20s. (2)

11. Clouds may become charged due to very small particles of ice rubbing against each other. In thunder clouds, the charge is greater than normal and lightning can occur.

(a) What is lightning? (2)

(b) The bottoms of thunder clouds gain a negative charge. Explain how lightning occurs. (4)

*12. Some buildings have a lightning conductor fixed to the outside wall. This is a copper rod that rises above the highest part of the building, with its lowest end connected to earth. Explain how this protects the building from lightning. (6)

*13. Describe the stages in the painting of a car using electrostatic charge. (6)

_____

_____

_____

_____

_____

_____

_____

_____

_____

_____

(Total: _____ / 51)

Higher Tier

14. A charge of 3.2×10^{-2} C flows when the current in a circuit is 0.014A. How long does the charge flow for? (2)

_____

_____

15. What current flows if a charge of 6.72×10^{-4} C flows for 23.5 seconds? (2)

_____

_____

(Total: _____ / 4)

Questions labelled with an asterisk (*) are ones where the quality of your written communication will be assessed – you should take particular care with your spelling, punctuation and grammar, as well as the clarity of expression, on these questions.

1. Draw the circuit diagrams in the spaces below.

   (a) A circuit with one cell and two lamps in series. (2)

   (b) A circuit with one cell and two lamps in parallel. (2)

2. The diagram below shows a simple circuit.

   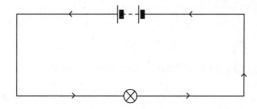

   Using the correct symbol, draw on the diagram where you would connect:

   (a) an ammeter in the circuit to measure the current (2)

   (b) a voltmeter in the circuit to measure the potential difference (voltage) across the lamp. (2)

3. The diagram below shows a circuit with two lamps in parallel. The current passing through the top lamp is 0.2A.

   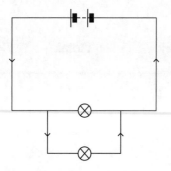

   (a) The bottom lamp is identical to the top lamp. What is the current passing through the bottom lamp? (1)

   _____

   (b) What is the total current passing through the rest of the circuit? (1)

   _____

4. A circuit has two cells connected in series with a lamp. How does the brightness of the lamp change if:

(a) one cell is removed? _____ (1)

(b) one cell is added so there are now three cells? _____ (1)

(c) (i) How does the brightness of the lamp depend on the number of cells? (2)

_____

(ii) How does the current in the circuit depend on the size of the voltage? (2)

_____

5. **(a) (i)** What does **resistance** mean in a circuit? (1)

_____

(ii) What unit is used to measure resistance? Give the full name and symbol. (1)

_____

(b) The resistance is increased in a circuit. How does this change the current? (1)

_____

(c) What component could be used in a circuit to change the resistance? (1)

_____

6. The graph below shows how the amount of light falling on a light-dependent resistor (LDR) affects its resistance.

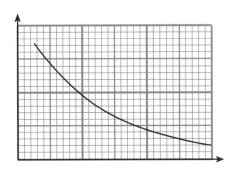

(a) Label the axes of the graph. (2)

(b) Explain the shape of the graph. (2)

_____

(c) Give **one** example of the use of an LDR. (1)

_____

7. **(a)** Sketch and label a graph to show the relationship between resistance and temperature for a thermistor. (3)

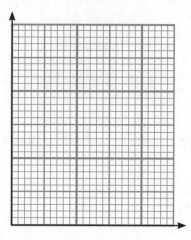

(b) In terms of resistance, thermistors are not like most electrical components, such as light bulbs. Explain why. In what ways is a thermistor like an LDR? (3)

....

....

....

8. **(a)** To calculate the potential difference across a component, what **two** things do you need to know?

(i) .... **(ii)** .... (2)

(b) In a series circuit, the reading on an ammeter is 0.6A. The total resistance is 10Ω. Calculate the potential difference supplied by the battery. (2)

....

....

9. In the circuits shown below, each cell provides a potential difference of 1.5V.

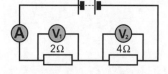 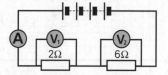 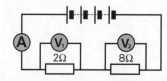

For each circuit, calculate the following: (For part **(iii)** you will need to use current = $\frac{V}{R}$)

(a) **(i)** p.d. supplied = ... **(b)** **(i)** p.d. supplied = ... **(c)** **(i)** p.d. supplied = ...

(ii) total resistance = ... **(ii)** total resistance = ... **(ii)** total resistance = ...

(iii) ammeter reading = ... **(iii)** ammeter reading = ... **(iii)** ammeter reading = ...

(iv) V_1 = ... **(iv)** V_1 = ... **(iv)** V_1 = ...

(v) V_2 = ... (3) **(v)** V_2 = ... (3) **(v)** V_2 = ... (3)

10. Josh decides to investigate how the current flowing through a filament bulb changes with the potential difference across it. He obtained the results below.

Potential Difference (V)	0.0	1.0	2.0	3.0	4.0	5.0
Current (A)	0.0	1.1	1.7	2.1	2.3	2.5

(a) On the graph paper below plot a current–potential difference graph. (4)

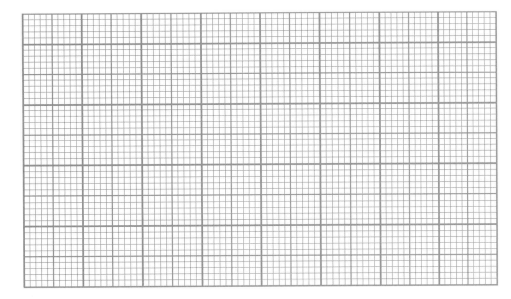

(b) (i) Describe the shape of your graph. (4)

....

....

....

....

(ii) Explain the shape of the graph. (2)

....

....

....

....

11. The graphs below show current against potential difference for different components.

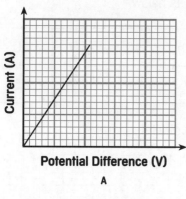

Current (A) vs Potential Difference (V)

A

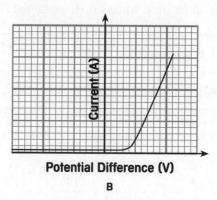

Current (A) vs Potential Difference (V)

B

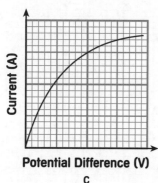

Current (A) vs Potential Difference (V)

C

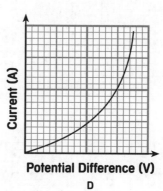

Current (A) vs Potential Difference (V)

D

(a) Which one shows the graph for a fixed resistor? .... (1)

(b) Which one shows the graph for a resistance that increases? .... (1)

(c) Which one shows the graph for a diode? .... (1)

12. An electric current passing through a wire causes it to heat up. Name a common electrical

device that makes use of this effect. .... (1)

13. In the device you wrote as the answer to question 12, there is a transfer of energy. What is the

main energy transfer that takes place? .... (2)

14. A similar device works on the mains voltage of 230V and draws a current of 5A.

(a) What is its power, in watts? .... (2)

(b) How much electrical energy is transferred in:

  (i) 1 second? .... (1)

  (ii) 1 minute? .... (2)

*15. Describe how you could carry out an experiment to show the relationship between potential difference and current for a light-dependent resistor when the intensity of the light incident on the LDR is varied. You may assume that normal laboratory equipment is available. (6)

....

....

....

....

....

....

....

(Total: .... / 71)

Higher Tier

16. **(a)** A current of 0.75A flows through a lamp. When a voltmeter is placed across the lamp to measure the potential difference, the current drops to 0.74A.

    (i) What current flows through the voltmeter? (1)

....

    (ii) What does this tell you about the relative size of its resistance? (2)

....

  (b) The voltmeter reads 3.4V.

    Calculate the resistance of the:

    (i) lamp (2)

....

    (ii) voltmeter. (2)

....

17. **(a)** In question 16, how much energy is transferred by the lamp per coulomb of charge passed? (1)

....

continued...

(b) If 15C passes through the lamp in a certain time, how much energy is transferred? (2)

18. What is the size of the current flowing in an ink-jet printer that has a power consumption of 30W, working on a mains voltage of 230V? (2)

19. A current of 4.7A is drawn by a laptop with a power output of 90W. What size voltage should the charger for the laptop provide? (2)

20. When a current flows through a resistor, there is an energy transfer.

    (a) What happens to the resistor? (1)

    (b) Explain, in terms of the movement of atoms and electrons, how this transfer of energy occurs. (4)

21. The energy transferred by a device is given by:

$$E = I \times V \times t$$

    (a) By thinking about the definition of potential difference in terms of amount of energy transferred per unit charge, derive the relation between charge, current and time. (3)

    (b) An electric kettle has a power consumption of 1100W.

    (i) How long does it take to transfer 25 000J? (1)

    (ii) Working on a mains voltage of 240V, what current does it draw? (2)

(Total: _____ / 25)

Questions labelled with an asterisk (*) are ones where the quality of your written communication will be assessed – you should take particular care with your spelling, punctuation and grammar, as well as the clarity of expression, on these questions.

1. Mandy is talking to a friend, trying to explain what is meant by the velocity of a car. (1)

A ◯ Velocity is the same as speed.

B ◯ Velocity is speed in two different directions.

C ◯ Velocity is speed in a certain direction.

D ◯ Velocity is the direction of the car.

2. A distance–time graph for a person walking along a road is shown below.

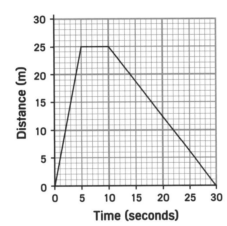

(a) Calculate the speed:

(i) in the first 5 seconds (2)

....

(ii) in the last 20 seconds. (2)

....

(b) What was the total distance walked? (1)

....

(c) Describe the journey that the person takes. (3)

....

....

3. A truck is stationary at a set of traffic lights. When the lights change, it moves off and reaches a velocity of 15m/s after 30s. Calculate the acceleration of the truck. (2)

....

....

4. Study the four velocity–time graphs below.

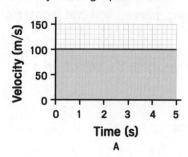

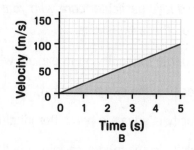

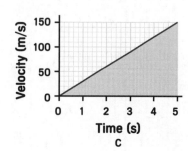

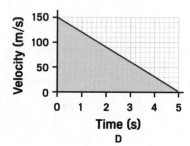

Which graphs **A**, **B**, **C** or **D** show:

(a) an object that is constantly decelerating? _____ (1)

(b) an object that has zero acceleration? _____ (1)

(c) an object that is constantly accelerating? _____ (1)

(d) an object that is moving at a steady velocity? _____ (1)

5. Calculate the acceleration shown in graph **C** of question 4. (2)

_____

6. A train is moving along a track.

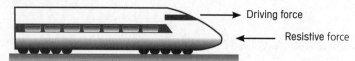

Describe the relationship between the two forces shown when: (1)

(a) the train accelerates

_____

(b) the train moves at constant speed (1)

_____

(c) the train slows down. (1)

_____

7. In free-body force diagrams, an arrow is used to show the direction of a force. The length of the arrow shows the size of the force. Draw a free-body force diagram for:

(a) a man standing on the ground (3)

(b) a hot air-balloon accelerating upwards. (3)

8. Calculate the weight in each of the following (taking g = 10N/kg).

(a) The mass of a girl is 45kg. (1)

(b) The mass of a car is 900kg. (1)

9. A car of mass 800kg accelerates at 1.5m/s². Calculate the driving force of the car. (2)

10. Use the formula: **acceleration = $\frac{\text{force}}{\text{mass}}$** in the following questions.

(a) A full supermarket trolley of total mass 25kg is pushed along with a resultant force of 10N. Calculate the acceleration. (1)

(b) A lorry of mass 2000kg has a driving force of 2800N. The resistive forces total 1800N.

    (i) What is the resultant driving force? (1)

    (ii) Calculate the acceleration. (1)

11. The drawing below shows the main forces acting on a skydiver. (1)

Which statement correctly describes the situation that is shown?

A ☐ Force P is weight and force Q is air resistance.

B ☐ Force P is air resistance and force Q is acceleration.

C ☐ Force P is acceleration and force Q is air resistance.

D ☐ Force P is air resistance and force Q is weight.

12. The velocity–time graph below shows the motion of a skydiver at 10s intervals after he steps out of the aeroplane.

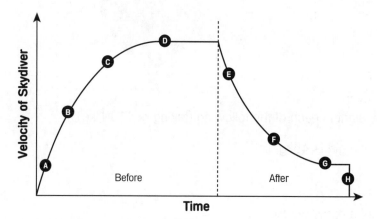

(a) Explain what happens at stages **A, B, C, and D**.

(i) A _____ (1)

(ii) B _____ (1)

(iii) C _____ (1)

(iv) D _____ (1)

(b) What stage does the dotted line represent? (1)

_____

(c) Explain what happens at stages **E, F, G, and H**.

(i) E _____ (1)

(ii) F _____ (1)

(iii) G _____ (1)

(iv) H _____ (1)

*13. In an investigation into the relationship between force, mass and acceleration of a trolley, the runway being used should be raised up so that the trolley runs down a slope.
Explain why this is necessary. Discuss this statement. (6)

(Total: .... / 49)

Higher Tier

14. A car travelling on a dual carriageway at constant velocity approaches a lorry just ahead. The car driver accelerates at 2m/s^2 for 5 seconds to overtake the lorry. The car reaches 90km/hr. What was its velocity in m/s just before it accelerated? (4)

15. A passenger train accelerates out of a station at 0.8m/s^2. If the driving force is 20000N, work out the mass of the train. (1)

16. A car moves with constant speed of 30m/s. The combined mass of car plus driver is 1000kg.

    (a) If the driving force is 3000N, what is the value of the resistive force? (1)

continued...

(b) If the driving force is increased to 4000N, calculate the acceleration of the car. (2)

(c) If the car accelerates for 20s at this acceleration. What will the velocity of the car be after this time? (2)

17. Look at the velocity–time graph, below, for a car's journey.

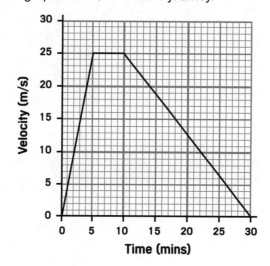

(a) What was the initial acceleration of the car? (2)

(b) What was the distance travelled at a constant velocity? (2)

(c) What was the total distance travelled? (2)

(d) What was the deceleration of the car on the final part of the journey? (2)

(e) What was the average velocity of the car for the whole journey? (2)

(Total: .... / 20)

Questions labelled with an asterisk (*) are ones where the quality of your written communication will be assessed – you should take particular care with your spelling, punctuation and grammar, as well as the clarity of expression, on these questions.

1. The total stopping distance of a vehicle is the sum of **two** distances. What are they called? (2)

   (a) _____ **(b)** _____

2. Which of the following conditions **will not** increase the stopping distance of a car? (1)

   A ◯ The car is travelling at high speed. C ◯ The road is dry.

   B ◯ It is raining hard. D ◯ The driver is sleepy.

3. A driver is driving steadily. She suddenly sees a child step out in front of her car. She brakes.

   (a) What is meant by the driver's 'reaction time'? (2)

   _____

   _____

   (b) Apart from feeling tired, name **two** other things that could increase reaction time.

   (i) _____ (1)

   (ii) _____ (1)

4. A woman is learning to drive. Her driving instructor points out the various features of the car. Below is a list of features. Which one is a safety feature? (1)

   A ◯ Sat-nav C ◯ Metallic paint

   B ◯ Air bag D ◯ Alloy wheels

5. What **two** things do you need to know to calculate the momentum of a vehicle? (2)

   (a) _____ **(b)** _____

6. A car of mass 1000kg travels at a constant velocity of 20m/s.

   (a) Calculate the momentum of the car. (2)

   _____

   (b) Another car of the same mass is travelling at the same velocity but in the **opposite** direction. What is the momentum of this car? (1)

   _____

7. Use the equation $\textbf{velocity} = \dfrac{\textbf{momentum}}{\textbf{mass}}$ to calculate the velocity of a motorbike if its mass is 250kg, the rider has a mass of 90kg and its momentum is 8500kg m/s. (3)

   _____

   _____

8. In a collision between two bodies, momentum is **conserved**.

(a) What does this mean? (1)

....

(b) Two cars are travelling in the same direction. They both have the same mass of 800kg.
The velocity of the one in front is 20m/s. The other is moving at 30m/s.

At some point, the cars will collide.

(i) Calculate the total momentum before they collide. (2)

....

....

(ii) Write down the total momentum after they collide. (1)

....

9. A cyclist moves along a level road against resistive forces of 150N. He travels 1500m.
Calculate the work done by the cyclist. (2)

....

10. A man lifts up a parcel of weight 50N from the ground through a distance of 1.8m. (2)

(a) How much work does he do?

....

(b) How much energy does he transfer? (1)

....

(c) Explain your answer to **(b)**. (1)

....

11. A crane on a building site lifts a load of 50 000N through a distance of 30m.

(a) Calculate the work done. (2)

....

(b) If this takes 20s, calculate the power output of the crane. (2)

....

12. **(a)** What is **gravitational potential energy** (GPE)? (1)

....

....

(b) Give **two** examples of objects that have GPE.

(i) .... (1)

(ii) .... (1)

13. A girl climbs 5m up a tree. Her mass is 50kg. Work out her gravitational potential energy. (2)

....

14. A football of mass 0.4kg is kicked into the air to a height of 8m.

(a) Calculate the gravitational potential energy that the ball gains. (2)

....

(b) What happens to this energy as the ball starts to fall back to the ground? (1)

....

15. Give **two** examples of objects that have kinetic energy.

(a) .... (1)

(b) .... (1)

16. A lorry of mass 2000kg moves at 20m/s. Calculate the kinetic energy of the lorry. (2)

....

....

17. Energy can only be transferred from one form to another. Draw a line to match each example to the correct description of how energy is transferred. (4)

(a) Using an iron	**(i)** Potential energy to kinetic energy to potential energy
(b) Speaking into a mobile phone	**(ii)** Kinetic energy to heat (thermal) energy
(c) A child on a park swing	**(iii)** Sound energy to electrical energy
(d) A car stopping at traffic lights	**(iv)** Electrical energy to heat (thermal) energy

*18. Outline an experiment you could perform in a school laboratory to investigate how the force needed to move a wooden block depends on the type of surface. (6)

_____

_____

_____

_____

_____

_____

_____

_____

_____

19. In terms of momentum change, explain how the air bags in a car protect the passengers. (3)

_____

_____

_____

20. The velocity-time graph below shows a car having to make an emergency stop.

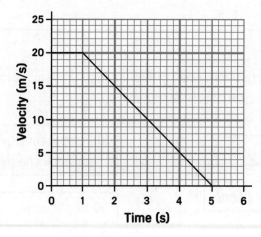

Use the graph to answer the following questions.

(a) How fast was the car travelling before it braked? _____ (1)

(b) What was the thinking distance? _____ (1)

(c) How long did it take the car to come to rest after the brakes were applied? (1)

_____

(d) What was the overall stopping distance? .... (1)

21. In a hydro-electric plant, 10^4 kg of water is pumped back up to the upper reservoir through a distance of 120m.

(a) Calculate the work done by the pumps. (2)

_____

(b) This process takes 3 minutes 20 seconds. Calculate the power output of the pumps. (2)

_____

22. Which of the following statements best describes the principle of the conservation of energy? Tick the correct statement. (1)

A ◯ Energy is constantly being lost, so new energy needs to be generated.

B ◯ New energy is constantly being formed, so the total amount of energy grows.

C ◯ Energy cannot be made, lost or transferred.

D ◯ It is only possible to transfer energy to different forms.

(Total: .... / 64)

Higher Tier

23. A train engine reverses on to a carriage to be attached to it. It exerts a force of 2000N over a period of 0.45s.

Calculate the change in momentum of the train and carriage. (4)

_____

_____

_____

_____

continued...

24. A car of mass 750kg is travelling at 20m/s. It is forced to slow suddenly to a velocity of 5m/s in a time of 5s.

(a) Calculate the change in momentum. (2)

(b) Now calculate the force exerted on the driver. (2)

25. **(a)** What is the relationship between a car's kinetic energy and the work done to stop it? (1)

(b) Hence show that the stopping distance of a car is proportional to the square of its velocity. (4)

(c) A lorry of mass 5000kg travelling at 25m/s brakes by applying a force of 10 000N. What is its stopping distance? (2)

*26. Habiba and Connor are talking about the stopping distance of a vehicle. Connor thinks that the stopping distance is directly proportional to speed because it takes more energy to stop it if it is moving faster. Habiba disagrees. She says that the stopping distance is much more at greater speeds, so it cannot be proportional to speed.

Who is right? Explain the physics behind your answer. (6)

(Total: .... / 21)

Nuclear Fission and Nuclear Fusion

Questions labelled with an asterisk (*) are ones where the quality of your written communication will be assessed – you should take particular care with your spelling, punctuation and grammar, as well as the clarity of expression, on these questions.

1. The diagram below shows a simple model of a lithium (Li) atom. Lithium has an atomic number of 3 and a mass number of 7.

    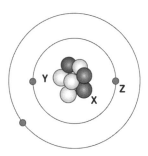

    Name the particles **X**, **Y** and **Z**.

    (a) X = _____   **(b)** Y = _____   (3)

    (c) Z = _____

2. The atomic number of cobalt is 27. Cobalt has two isotopes, cobalt-60 and cobalt-59.

    (a) What is an isotope?   (2)

    _____

    _____

    (b) Fill in the missing information about the two isotopes of cobalt to complete the table below.   (3)

	Cobalt-60	Cobalt-59
(i) Number of protons		
(ii) Number of neutrons		
(iii) Number of electrons		

3. The various isotopes of an element, X, are written in the following way: $_{Z}^{A}X$

    What do the letters A and Z represent?   (2)

    A = _____

    Z = _____

4. Lithium can be represented as $_{3}^{7}Li$

    Represent cobalt-60 and cobalt-59 in the same way.   (2)

    Cobalt-60 _____   Cobalt-59 _____

5. What do we mean if we say that a substance is **radioactive**? (1)

6. Draw lines to link each different type of radiation to the relevant description/s. A description can apply to more than one type of radiation. (3)

(i) Emitted from a nucleus

(ii) Very high-frequency radiation

(a) Alpha

(iii) Consists of two protons and two neutrons

(b) Beta

(iv) Very short wavelength radiation

(c) Gamma

(v) Fast-moving electron

(vi) Has a negative charge

(vii) A helium nucleus

7. Alpha, beta and gamma radiation are directed at three absorbers, as shown below.

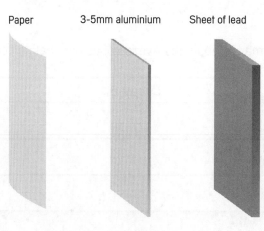

Paper   3-5mm aluminium   Sheet of lead

(a) Which radiation or radiations will still be detected after going through the sheet of paper? (1)

(b) Which absorbers will not let beta radiation through them? (1)

(c) Which radiation or radiations will still be detected after passing through the lead? (1)

8. Alpha, beta and gamma radiation are all said to be ionising radiations.

(a) What is the meaning of **ionise** or **ionising**? (3)

....

....

(b) These radiations have different ionising powers. Which radiation has the strongest ionising

power? .... (1)

9. Nuclear fission and nuclear fusion are processes that release large amounts of energy.
What is the difference between them? (4)

Nuclear fission ....

....

Nuclear fusion ....

....

10. The diagram below shows part of a nuclear fission process. Write the following labels in the
correct places on the diagram. (4)

energy   neutron   unstable nucleus   fission occurs
further neutrons   uranium nucleus   new radioactive nuclei are formed

11. Chain reactions can be **controlled** or **uncontrolled**. Give an example of:

(a) a controlled chain reaction .... (1)

(b) an uncontrolled chain reaction. .... (1)

(c) Name the **two** methods of controlling a chain reaction.

(i) .... (1)

(ii) .... (1)

12. Below is a diagram of a type of nuclear reactor.

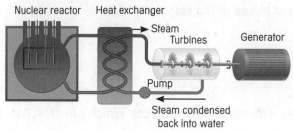

Explain how electricity is produced from a nuclear reactor. (4)

....

....

....

....

....

....

....

13. An unstable nucleus emits radiation at **random**. What do you understand by this? (1)

....

14. (a) What are the products of nuclear fission? (3)

....

....

(b) Are these products radioactive or non-radioactive? (1)

....

(c) What potential problem does this pose? (1)

....

....

15. Once nuclear fission has started, it continues by itself.

(a) What is the term used to describe a self-sustaining reaction like this? (1)

....

(b) Describe how this reaction continues. (3)

16. What is the difference between a **controlled** and an **uncontrolled** chain reaction? (4)

Controlled

Uncontrolled

17. Explain what happens during the nuclear fusion process. (3)

18. Name and explain **two** conditions that must be met before nuclear fusion can occur.

(a) (3)

(b) (3)

(c) Where in the Universe are these conditions met?

(1)

19. Using the words below, label the diagram appropriately to show a nuclear fusion reaction. (3)

deuterium   helium   tritium   energy   neutron   **fusion occurs**

....

....

....

....

....

(Total: .... / 66)

Higher Tier

20. Explain the **three** practical problems involved in producing energy from nuclear fusion.

(a) .... (2)

....

(b) .... (2)

....

(c) .... (2)

....

*21. Explain the theory of **cold fusion**. Why is this not an accepted theory? (6)

....

....

....

....

....

....

....

....

....

(Total: .... / 12)

Questions labelled with an asterisk (*) are ones where the quality of your written communication will be assessed – you should take particular care with your spelling, punctuation and grammar, as well as the clarity of expression, on these questions.

1. What is meant by **background radiation**? (1)

A ◯ Radiation that is produced by someone working in the background.

B ◯ Radiation that occurs from the fall-out of atomic bombs.

C ◯ Radiation that occurs in the environment.

D ◯ Radiation that occurs from outer space.

2. The following are some of the sources of background radiation.

radon gas   **nuclear industry**   **cosmic rays**   **gamma rays**

(a) Name **one** other source. (1)

....

(b) Which one of the above sources contributes most to background radiation? (1)

....

3. Name **two** uses of radioactivity.

(a) .... (1)

(b) .... (1)

4. **(a)** What is meant by the half-life of a radioactive source? (3)

....

....

....

....

(b) A radioactive source has a half-life of 1 hour. Its activity is measured as 1600Bq at 9 a.m. What would its activity be at:

(i) 10 a.m.? (1)

....

(ii) 12 p.m.? (1)

....

(c) At what time would its activity be 25Bq? (1)

....

5. The explosion at the Chernobyl Nuclear Reactor released a large cloud of radioactive gas into the atmosphere that spread over Europe. The gas contained caesium-137 (with a half-life of 30 years) and iodine-131. The following table shows measurements of the count rate, in bequerels, from a small amount of iodine-131.

Time (days)	0	4	8	12
Count Rate (Bq)	320	250	160	125

(a) From the table above, work out the half-life of iodine-131. (1)

*(b)** Four months after the explosion, scientists were no longer concerned about the health risks from the iodine but were still worried about the effects of the caesium-137. Do you think that they were right to be concerned about the caesium but not about the iodine? Explain your answer. (6)

6. (a) Americium-241 is used in smoke detectors. It has a half-life of 460 years. How long will it take for the number of radioactive atoms in a sample of Americium-241 to decrease to $\frac{1}{8}$ of the original number? (2)

(b) Do you think that it is a good idea to use a radioactive isotope with such a long half-life? Explain your answer. (1)

7. Why is ionising radiation dangerous to humans? (2)

8. The damaging effects of radiation depend on whether the radiation source is outside or inside the body.

(a) Which type/s of ionising radiation is not harmful to the inside of the body when the source is outside? Explain your answer. (2)

(b) Which types of ionising radiation are less harmful when the source is inside the body? Explain your answer. (2)

9. A nurse is delivering radiotherapy to a patient. What type of precautions should she take:

   (a) for her own protection? (1)

   (b) for her patient's protection? (1)

10. In 1901, radium was first used to treat patients with cancerous tumours.

    (a) Radium-based paint was invented a few years later. What was it used for? (1)

    (b) Why were substances containing radium removed from use in the 1930s? (1)

11. State **two** advantages and **two** disadvantages of using nuclear power to generate electricity.

    Advantages: (2)

    Disadvantages: (2)

12. There are **three** different types of nuclear waste.

    (a) What are they? (1)

    (b) (i) Which one is the most common type that has to be dealt with? (1)

(ii) Where does this waste come from? (2)

_____

_____

13. The graph below shows the decay of a radioactive isotope.

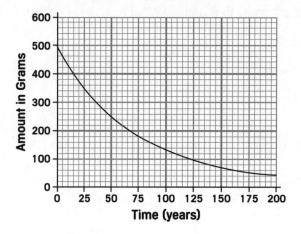

(a) What is the average half-life of this material? (1)

....

(b) What fraction of the material would remain after 300 years? (1)

....

14. A smoke alarm makes use of a radioactive isotope. The diagram below shows a simple smoke detector.

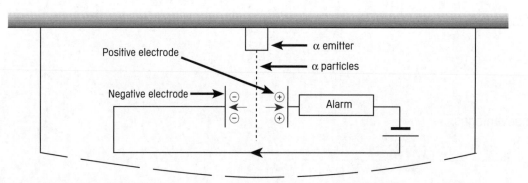

(a) Give **two** reasons why a source emitting alpha particles, rather than beta or gamma rays, is used. (2)

_____

_____

_____

(b) Explain how the smoke alarm works. (4)

15. Part of the skeleton of an animal is unearthed in an archaeological dig. A Geiger counter measures the activity of radioactive carbon-14 present as 450Bq. Over the same period of time, the same mass of new bone has an average activity of about 1740Bq.

(a) Calculate the approximate age of the skeleton, given that the half-life of carbon-14 is 5730 years. (2)

(b) (i) Why is your answer only an approximation? (1)

(ii) Should the actual age be more or less than the answer you gave in **(a)**? (1)

16. One disadvantage of using nuclear power for electricity generation is the waste produced.

(a) Where does high-level waste come from and what can be done about it in the short and long term? (4)

(b) Other waste accounts for nearly all of the waste produced.

(i) Why is it not as dangerous as high-level waste? (1)

(ii) What is done with this kind of waste? (3)

(Total: .... / 59)

Formulae Sheet

C2

Formulae of Some Common Ions

Positive Ions		Negative Ions	
Name	**Formula**	**Name**	**Formula**
Hydrogen	H^+	Chloride	Cl^-
Sodium	Na^+	Bromide	Br^-
Silver	Ag^+	Fluoride	F^-
Potassium	K^+	Iodide	I^-
Lithium	Li^+	Hydroxide	OH^-
Ammonium	NH_4^+	Nitrate	NO_3^-
Barium	Ba^{2+}	Oxide	O^{2-}
Calcium	Ca^{2+}	Sulfide	S^{2-}
Copper (II)	Cu^{2+}	Sulfate	SO_4^{2-}
Magnesium	Mg^{2+}	Carbonate	CO_3^{2-}
Zinc	Zn^{2+}		
Lead	Pb^{2+}		
Iron (II)	Fe^{2+}		
Iron (III)	Fe^{3+}		
Aluminium	Al^{3+}		

$$\text{Percentage yield} = \frac{\text{mass of product obtained}}{\text{maximum theoretical mass of product}} \times 100\%$$

$$\text{Atom economy} = \frac{\text{mass of wanted product from equation}}{\text{total mass of products from equation}} \times 100\%$$

$$\text{Molecular formula} = \frac{\text{empirical formula} \times M_r}{M_r \text{ of empirical formula}}$$

$$\text{Percentage by mass of an element in a compound} = \frac{\text{relative mass of all the atoms of that element}}{M_r} \times 100\%$$

$$\text{Rate of reaction} = \frac{\text{amount of reactant used}}{\text{time}}$$

$$\text{Rate of reaction} = \frac{\text{amount of product formed}}{\text{time}}$$

Formulae Sheet

P2

Charge (coulomb, C) = current (ampere, A) × time (second, s) $Q = I \times t$

Potential difference (volt, V) = current (ampere, A) × resistance (ohm, Ω) $V = I \times R$

Electrical power (watt, W) = current (ampere, A) × potential difference (volt, V) $P = I \times V$

Energy transferred (joule, J) = current (ampere, A) × potential difference (volt, V) × time (second, s) $E = I \times V \times t$

Speed (metre per second, m/s) = $\dfrac{\text{distance (metre, m)}}{\text{time (second, s)}}$

Acceleration (metre per second squared, m/s²) = $\dfrac{\text{change in velocity (metre per second, m/s)}}{\text{time taken (second, s)}}$ $a = \dfrac{(v - u)}{t}$

Force (newton, N) = mass (kilogram, kg) × acceleration (metre per second squared, m/s²) $F = m \times a$

Weight (newton, N) = mass (kilogram, kg) × gravitational field strength (newton per kilogram, N/kg) $W = m \times g$

momentum (kilogram metre per second, kg m/s) = mass (kilogram, kg) × velocity (metre per second, m/s) $momentum = m \times v$

Work done (joule, J) = force (newton, N) × distance moved in the direction of the force (metre, m) $E = F \times d$

Power (watt, W) = $\dfrac{\text{work done (joule, J)}}{\text{time taken (second, s)}}$ $P = \dfrac{E}{t}$

Gravitational potential energy (joule, J) = mass (kilogram, kg) × gravitational field strength (newton per kilogram, N/kg) × vertical height (metre, m)
$GPE = m \times g \times h$

Kinetic energy (joule, J) = $\dfrac{1}{2}$ × mass (kilogram, kg) × velocity² ([metre/second]² [m/s]²) $KE = \dfrac{1}{2} \times m \times v^2$

Higher Tier

Force (newton, N) = $\dfrac{\text{change in momentum (kilogram metre per second, kg m/s)}}{\text{time (second, s)}}$ $F = \dfrac{(mv - mu)}{t}$

Periodic Table

Key

relative atomic mass
atomic symbol
name
atomic (proton) number

| 1 | H hydrogen 1 |

*The lanthanoids (atomic numbers 58–71) and the actinoids (atomic numbers 90–103) have been omitted.

The relative atomic masses of copper and chlorine have not been rounded to the nearest whole number.

Elements with atomic numbers 112–116 have been reported but not fully authenticated.

1	2											3	4	5	6	7	0
																	4 **He** helium 2
7 **Li** lithium 3	9 **Be** beryllium 4											11 **B** boron 5	12 **C** carbon 6	14 **N** nitrogen 7	16 **O** oxygen 8	19 **F** fluorine 9	20 **Ne** neon 10
23 **Na** sodium 11	24 **Mg** magnesium 12											27 **Al** aluminium 13	28 **Si** silicon 14	31 **P** phosphorus 15	32 **S** sulfur 16	35.5 **Cl** chlorine 17	40 **Ar** argon 18
39 **K** potassium 19	40 **Ca** calcium 20	45 **Sc** scandium 21	48 **Ti** titanium 22	51 **V** vanadium 23	52 **Cr** chromium 24	55 **Mn** manganese 25	56 **Fe** iron 26	59 **Co** cobalt 27	59 **Ni** nickel 28	63.5 **Cu** copper 29	65 **Zn** zinc 30	70 **Ga** gallium 31	73 **Ge** germanium 32	75 **As** arsenic 33	79 **Se** selenium 34	80 **Br** bromine 35	84 **Kr** krypton 36
85 **Rb** rubidium 37	88 **Sr** strontium 38	89 **Y** ytrium 39	91 **Zr** zirconium 40	93 **Nb** niobium 41	96 **Mo** molybdenum 42	[98] **Tc** technetium 43	101 **Ru** ruthenium 44	103 **Rh** rhodium 45	106 **Pd** palladium 46	108 **Ag** silver 47	112 **Cd** cadmium 48	115 **In** indium 49	119 **Sn** tin 50	122 **Sb** antimony 51	128 **Te** tellurium 52	127 **I** iodine 53	131 **Xe** xenon 54
133 **Cs** caesium 55	137 **Ba** barium 56	139 **La*** lanthanum 57	178 **Hf** hafnium 72	181 **Ta** tantalum 73	184 **W** tungsten 74	186 **Re** rhenium 75	190 **Os** osmium 76	192 **Ir** iridium 77	195 **Pt** platinum 78	197 **Au** gold 79	201 **Hg** mercury 80	204 **Tl** thallium 81	207 **Pb** lead 82	209 **Bi** bismuth 83	[209] **Po** polonium 84	[210] **At** astatine 85	[222] **Rn** radon 86
[223] **Fr** francium 87	[226] **Ra** radium 88	[227] **Ac*** actinium 89	[261] **Rf** rutherfordium 104	[262] **Db** dubnium 105	[266] **Sg** seaborgium 106	[264] **Bh** bohrium 107	[277] **Hs** hassium 108	[268] **Mt** meitnerium 109	[271] **Ds** darmstadtium 110	[272] **Rg** roentgenium 111							

Notes

Notes